RICE

Jerry Rice and Michael Silver

ST. MARTIN'S PRESS
New York

AN OPUS BOOK

To the most courageous person I know — my wife, Jackie.

Her strength and tenacity truly make her a world champion.

She motivates our entire family — Jaqui, Jerry Jr., and Jada —

to make each day count.

I love you Jackie, and thanks for being my very best friend.

RICE. © Copyright 1996 by Jerry Rice and Opus Productions Inc.

All rights reserved. Printed in the United States of America. No part of this book may be used or reproduced in any manner whatsoever without written permission except in the case of brief quotations embodied in critical articles or reviews. For information, address St. Martin's Press, 175 Fifth Avenue, New York, N.Y. 10010. The publishers do not assume responsibility for the historical accuracy of the information contained in this book.

Created and produced by Opus Productions Inc., 300 West Hastings Street, Vancouver, British Columbia, Canada V6B 1K6

Library of Congress Cataloging-in-Publication Data:
Rice, Jerry.
        Rice / by Jerry Rice and Michael Silver.
        p.   cm.
        ISBN 0-312-14795-3 (pbk)
        ISBN 0-312-14796-1 (hc)
        1. Rice, Jerry, 1962- . 2. Football players–United States–Biography.
        3. San Francisco 49ers (Football team)   I. Silver, Michael, 1965- .
        II. Title
GV939.R53A3 1996
796.332'092 B–dc20   96-8685
                                                                      CIP

First Edition: October 1996
10 9 8 7 6 5 4 3 2 1

TABLE OF CONTENTS

Introduction

The conversation wasn't meant for my ears, but it was hard to avoid, being in a public establishment and all. It could have taken place in any bar in any city where football is held dear. This particular debate happened in Pittsburgh on a nippy January afternoon in 1995.

"I'd have to pick Raymond Berry," growled Mac The Bartender. "He had the sweetest hands of anybody, and he won all those big games with Johnny Unitas in Baltimore."

"I'll go with Lance Alworth," Iron Ike interrupted. "Bambi could run and jump like no one, he had incredible numbers, and he carried the AFL on his back."

Football Fannie shook her head vigorously: "You want to talk sheer talent? What about Warfield, or Maynard, or our own Lynn Swann?"

"You're all crazy," Norm declared, "because there's only one receiver worth discussing here – Don Hutson of the old Green Bay Packers, and let me tell you why: From 1935 to '45, Hutson had three times as many touchdowns, and more than twice as many receptions, as the next best pass-catcher. He dominated his sport as much as Babe Ruth dominated baseball."

I was about to scream out, "Jerry Rice! Are you all nuts? Jerry Rice!" Then it occurred to me that Rice's name had not come up for a very legitimate reason, one which was made obvious when I heard Pigskin Pete's squeaky voice emanating from the shuffleboard table. "I've got to agree with Norm," he said. "Don Hutson is absolutely, positively the second-greatest receiver of all time."

That's how obvious it is that Jerry Rice is the greatest wide receiver in football history. In 11 seasons with the San Francisco 49ers, he has redefined his craft, catching more passes for more yards and more touchdowns than anyone who has ever lived. Rice has been an NFL Most Valuable Player and a Super Bowl MVP. He owns every meaningful career receiving record, and he has played his best in his biggest games. In three Super Bowls, all of which the 49ers won, Rice has averaged 9.3 catches, 170.7 yards and 2.3 touchdowns.

In some ways, Rice has been blessed. His 6-2, 185-pound frame moves swiftly and gracefully. His large, soft hands look made for catching footballs. He entered the National Football League with a team quarterbacked by Joe Montana, the greatest quarterback of all time, and later by Steve Young, another potential Hall of Famer.

But Rice has also thrived when teamed with less-decorated passers like Jeff Kemp, Elvis Grbac, and Steve Bono. Hell, he could probably make Sonny Bono look like an NFL quarterback. To call Rice blessed is to miss the point, for while his talents are enormous, they pale in comparison to his drive. Forged along the muddy dirt roads of Mississippi, fine-tuned in the hills of Northern California, Rice's work ethic and maniacal competitive edge have carried him beyond all previously established standards of excellence. His incredible mettle has allowed him to survive 18 seasons of organized football without ever having missed a game.

Even without this indefatigable intensity, Rice might be a good player, even a great one. But the reason he's the best is simple: He is the hardest working man in throw business.

He can be surly at times, but Rice is also sensitive, passionate, and relentlessly respectful. He brings a dignity to the game, one best reflected by the things he does not do: get into trouble off the field; taunt, flaunt, or showboat on it. His typical touchdown celebration is unfettered yet restrained. He acts like he has been there before, and he has: 156 end-zone trips entering the 1996 season, 30 more than anyone else in history. In a time when so many athletes fail to live up to their status as would-be heroes, Rice stands out as someone who conducts himself with aplomb on and off the field and who represents society's most cherished values: success through hard work, treating your peers and your opponents with respect, accepting responsibility for your actions.

Over the past seven years, as a beat writer covering the 49ers for newspapers in Northern California and as a senior writer for *Sports Illustrated*, I've had the opportunity to observe Rice's greatness from a privileged vantage point. I've seen shouting matches and outbursts, jeers and tears, humility and apologies, compassion and passion. I've also seen a man who, when all is said and done, may go down as the best football player of all time, period. If you don't believe me, take it from the man who drafted him, Hall of Fame coach Bill Walsh, who frames Rice's place in history this way: "I think if you name the five best players of all time, he'd be one of them, and then it would be up to people to pick their preference. But you couldn't find a better football player than Jerry Rice."

Michael Silver, Oakland, California, 1996

Facing page: *Definitely room on these hands for more: Jerry Rice with rings from his Super Bowl victories to date.*

Passion Plays

Far above the parched patches of Southwestern acreage, on a DC-10 alive with the sound of music and laughter, the greatest receiver of all time sat motionless and moist-eyed, a man alone in his despair. The San Francisco

Facing page: *Jerry Rice has provided the 49ers with countless moments of unequaled brilliance, but what truly sets him apart is his refusal to accept anything short of complete commitment.*
Above: Sport Magazine *Trophy awarded to Rice as the MVP of Super Bowl XXIII.*

49ers were flying home from Dallas on a chilly evening in January 1994, a few hours removed from a defeat that left the franchise in tatters. For the second consecutive year, the Dallas Cowboys had defeated the 49ers in the NFC Championship game and kept them from reaching the Super Bowl, this time by a 38-21 margin that probably should have been worse. No man hates losing more than Jerry Rice, but the sheer agony of defeat was not what drove him to such despair. This was the low point of his football career.

The 49ers had been called out by the Cowboys in the newspapers and in pregame warm-ups. In the game, Rice and his teammates had been pulverized. Things had gotten out of hand early. For one of the few times in his career, Rice had lost his cool, earning a personal foul penalty for throwing a forearm shiver at corner-back Kevin Smith. No one could question the great receiver's commit-ment, but in the heat of battle, with the Super Bowl on the line, many of his teammates, Rice felt, had failed to make the necessary sacrifices.

Now, as the gray winter horizon turned to black, Rice heard some of those same players clowning around in the back of the team plane, exuding youthful verve at a wholly inappro-priate time. He first felt ire, then disgust, and then he was crying and questioning everything he knew to be reality. After several minutes, he tempered his sobbing and tapped teammate and close friend Jamie Williams on the shoulder. "What's up?" asked Williams, a tight end who had just completed his 10th NFL season.

"That's some B.S., man," Rice said, gesturing toward the noisy players behind him. "These young guys, I just can't handle their attitude. They make me want to retire.

Here we just lost a chance to play in the Super Bowl and they're fooling around in the back. That they can't take this stuff seriously and give all they've got for what all this means, I just can't take it. It makes me want to not play anymore. I can't play with people like that."

Williams tried to calm his friend, to restore per-spective. Rice had already won two Super Bowl rings, once earning Most Valuable Player honors, the other time catching three touchdown passes. Soon he would own every meaningful NFL receiving record. The guys making noise in the back weren't such bad people; they just didn't understand. "I'll never forget that scene, because it was so poignant," Williams recalls. "Here's Jerry Rice, the greatest receiver of all time, a guy who's on the express elevator to the Hall of Fame, and he's just sitting there crying his eyes out. Here is a guy who understands what losing is – that it's something that eats at you, like a cancer. And there just weren't enough people around him who shared that understanding."

Rice got over his misery – indeed, he went on to win a third Super Bowl the following season, then put up perhaps his finest individual campaign the next year – but the memory of that flight lingers: "I don't think some of the guys realized what had just happened. Man, we went out and got our butts kicked. I didn't see anything to laugh about coming back on the plane. Nothing at all."

After sharing his thoughts with Williams, Rice closed his eyes and remembered the way it used to be back in the eighties. When the 49ers lost a big game – hell, any game – there was complete silence, from the time they reached the locker room to the moment their plane

Above: *Nobody in the NFL takes defeat harder than Jerry Rice. Angered by Dallas coach Jimmy Johnson's pre-game victory guarantee, Rice and the 49ers hoped to come charging out of the gate for the 1993 NFC Championship game.* **Facing page:** *Rice's world was turned upside down as he was tormented by the Cowboys on the field and by his teammates' indifference on the flight home.*

touched down. Losing was considered intolerable; this was one reason the 49ers, since the start of the eighties, had become the most successful franchise in professional sports.

When Rice first joined the team in 1985, veteran players like Joe Montana, Ronnie Lott, Dwight Clark, Keena Turner, and Freddie Solomon commanded so much respect that the rookies dared not risk their disapproval. Now Rice was the decorated veteran, the soul and conscience of his team, and he was appalled by the insolence in his midst. His best effort had come up short; his competitive fire had been futile. All the rigorous off-season workouts, all the fervent pregame focus, had essentially been wasted. "He was both irate and depressed," recalls 49ers president Carmen Policy. "He takes losing very badly. He can handle losing, in a professional sense, when he feels everybody's given his best, and if it's just not good enough to beat the opposition because the opposition's better, he can deal with that. But he can be a raving maniac at times, even if we've won, when he feels the team just didn't play the way it should be playing."

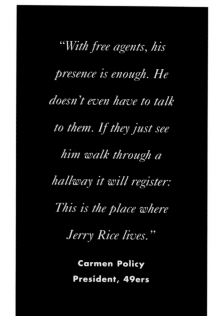

"With free agents, his presence is enough. He doesn't even have to talk to them. If they just see him walk through a hallway it will register: This is the place where Jerry Rice lives."

Carmen Policy
President, 49ers

So as the boomboxes blared and the jumbo jet began its descent, Rice decided enough was enough. Searing thoughts raced through his mind. *Football means so much to me. When I'm out there, it's everything. It's something you have to commit to, almost like a marriage, or it's just not worth it. If these guys aren't gonna give 100 percent, screw it. I don't need this anymore.*

If he could have right there, Rice would have torn up his contract, walked away from the millions and the adulation, and moved on with his life. And who could have questioned him? He had a great family, a lovely wife, and two wonderful children. His place in history was secure.

Quitting would have been a perfectly rational decision. But since when was Jerry Rice rational? This is a guy who works as hard in March as he does in November, a fitness fiend who refuses to ease up on his grueling workouts even when no one is watching. If there's a challenge to be met, Rice instinctively goes on the attack. When Rice got back to San Francisco, he started wondering what the 49ers needed to do to reach the top. He and his family went to Starkville, Mississippi – near Crawford, where he grew up – for a few weeks of relaxation with family and friends. Except Jerry couldn't relax. He ran mile after mile through the muddy fields he once roamed as a boy, the best receiver of all time trying to get even better.

Sometimes Rice would go out in public; that was the hardest part. As proud as the locals are of their home-town hero, Mississippi is Cowboys country. Growing up, Rice was a Dallas fan, and many of his friends back home still root for America's Team. Rice could handle their razzing. It was harder to hear taunts from the mouths of strangers. "Dall-ass, Dall-ass," they would chant. "They kicked your butt," others would yell. Rice had no response. At least, not yet. His answer would come later. From the singe he felt inside, he knew there was no way he could quit.

The next September, in the 49ers' first game of the season, Rice caught three touchdown passes in a 44-14 thrashing of the Raiders to break Jim Brown's all-time record of 126 visits to the end zone. In November, the 49ers beat the Cowboys at Candlestick Park, 21-14, and

Facing page: *The 49ers and Rice fought back in '94, twice beating the Cowboys en route to their fifth Super Bowl triumph.*
Following pages: *With Young, Rice would go on to set NFL single-game, season, and career receiving records.*

went on to earn the best regular-season record in football. In January, they met Dallas for the NFC Championship for the third consecutive year, again at Candlestick. This time, Rice caught the touchdown pass that broke the Cowboys' spirit, cradling a 28-yard toss from Steve Young in the corner of the end zone eight seconds before halftime for a 31-14 lead. The 49ers rolled to a 38-28 victory and went on to pummel San Diego in the Super Bowl, with Rice catching 10 passes for 149 yards.

When he visited Mississippi over the next off-season, Rice didn't get any flak from Cowboys fans. But the past wounds — particularly the one that had been opened in January of 1994 — had not completely healed. "You never get over it," Rice says. "You might put it behind you, but it's always going to be in the back of your head."

This is what makes Jerry Rice JERRY RICE: Unbridled passion, a raw faith in the purity of hard work, a gnawing fear of failure, and a fierce pride in himself and his teammates.

"I think he feels like he has to compensate for a lack of commitment from the younger guys. He has to keep the motor going. He not only has to drive, he has to navigate."

**Jamie Williams,
Tight End, 49ers
1989-93**

Facing page: *Playing the Cowboys at Texas Stadium always gives Rice a special charge. Here, on November 12, 1995, he outruns Larry Brown (24) and the rest of the Cowboys on his way to an 81-yard touchdown catch that sparked the 49ers' 38-20 victory.*

Striding Toward Success

When they were kids, Tom and Jerry Rice made a pact together: One of them would make it as a professional athlete in football or basketball – not baseball, because Jerry

Facing page: *Raw talent and a fierce work ethic helped Rice move from small-town Crawford to small-school stardom at Mississippi Valley State, where no. 88 was always on the run.* **Above:** *The Mississippi Valley State University MVP Trophy awarded to Jerry Rice.*

couldn't hit a curve ball – and reward their parents, Joe and Eddie B., with a brand-new house.

To understand the essence of Jerry Rice, you have to visit Crawford, Mississippi, but be careful not to blink. It's a town so small it makes Andy Griffith's Mayberry look like Manhattan. There were fewer than 500 residents when Rice was blossoming into a football star at Moor High School. A 40-foot-long house trailer parked in the town center served as a combination city hall, fire department, and public library.

Rice's father, Joe, and his mother, Eddie B. (pronounced Eddibee), raised eight children on a seven-acre spread in the countryside near Crawford proper. Jerry, their sixth child, born October 13, 1962, didn't talk much and rarely sat still. "He was very shy," says Eddie B. (The B doesn't stand for anything, like the S in Harry S. Truman.) "He didn't have much to say. He liked to run around and do a lot of exercising. He was very jumpy."

Rice and his siblings ran wild through the muggy, muddy heartland of eastern Mississippi. They did their share of horseback riding, but these were no ponies at the amusement park. In order to mount the horses that also ran wild in a big pasture on their property, Rice remembers, "We had to chase them down first, and it took 45 minutes to an hour at times, but we got rewarded because we'd ride them for the rest of the day.

"I prefer to ride bareback. In the saddle, it's too bouncy for me, too noisy. But bareback, it's just you and the horse. If the horse has a real smooth gallop it's just like riding on nothing – like riding on the wind."

Even at a young age, Jerry ran like the wind. He excelled in what might be called sandlot football games,

except they were played in dusty pastures. He ran in track meets on Saturdays. He was a talented basketball player, and he loved watching football on TV, admiring acrobatic receivers like Pittsburgh's Lynn Swann, and Drew Pearson of his beloved Cowboys. In a variation of the old theme, Jerry someday will be able to tell his three kids in all truthfulness, "I ran four miles home from school on sweltering dirt roads after practice." But in his first year at Moor High, Rice didn't play on the football team. "I didn't want him to play," his mother explains. "That was a rough team, and I didn't like football, period. I still don't like it – he's so skinny, and all those big men are out there hitting him when he jumps up for the ball."

It took a quirk of fate to get Rice into a football uniform, during his sophomore year. Rice was accustomed to obeying rules, if only to avoid the stern reproach of his parents. "Growing up in a small town taught me the meaning of doing the right things," he says. "Because the town was so small, if you did something wrong it was gonna get back to your parents. And with my parents, that meant you would be disciplined, so I think it made me into a better person. There was a lot of bad stuff going around – kids stealing cars, doing drugs – but I feel that my parents raised me the right way. We didn't have all the money, we didn't have all the luxuries, but I think because we were so close it made up for all that. I think my upbringing molded me into the person I am today."

No kid is perfect, however, and as a 10th grader, Rice would sometimes play hooky. He had a spot behind a building at the school where he could hide, but one day the principal went on a campus sweep and snuck up behind Jerry. The footsteps startled the class-cutter, who

Above: *Rice grew up in the countryside near Crawford, a tiny agricultural town in eastern Mississippi.*
Facing page: *Family Values: The strengths of a solid upbringing have served Rice well throughout his life, and kept him close to his roots. Back row from left: Tom, Joe Nathan, Sr., Joe Nathan, Jr., James, and Jimmy. Middle row from left: Loistine, Eddie Dean, and Eddie B. Front row: Zebedee (second from left) and Jerry (third from right), with younger nieces and nephews.*

"It's hard to find time to spend with my brothers and sisters now, but we still talk, and the relationships are still close when I go back home. I'm just Jerry, and that's really the way I like to be treated."

Jerry Rice

sped around the corner and dashed out of sight. All the principal saw was the blur of Rice's red blazer, but that was enough. When Jerry got to school the next morning, two things awaited him: a trip to the principal's office, and a mandate to join the football team.

"My punishment was that I got whipped, five or six times, with this thick strap that he had, and man was it painful," Rice recalls. "The principal's name was Ezel Wickes. I can't believe I can still remember his name, but I guess when someone gives you five or six lashes, you don't forget. He also reported me to the football coach because he saw how fast I was, and that was the beginning. I think everything happens for a reason. I was in the wrong place and I was not doing the right thing, and I really deserved to be punished."

The football team, which played at a "stadium" that seated only 100 people and had light poles on just one side of the field, served as a forum for Rice to display his tremendous work habits. As much as his childhood was filled with play, Rice always had a keen sense of the value of hard work.

As a child, he and his brothers and sisters picked corn and cotton to help their parents make ends meet. There were plenty of mouths for Joe Nathan and Eddie B. to feed: eldest daughter Eddie Dean, sons Joe Nathan, Jr., Tom, Jimmy, James, and Jerry, daughter Loistine, and youngest son Zebedee. As Jerry got older and began running in track meets on Saturdays, he would scramble to do his chores, most of them in the garden and the yard, before the weekend arrived.

But it wasn't until he became a teenager that Jerry truly ascertained the meaning of vocational dedication. It was then that his father, a bricklayer, began including him

on jobs during the summer months. Jerry and his four older brothers worked long hours at low wages, often leaving for work at 7 a.m. and getting home at 5 p.m. Then, Eddie B. remembers, Jerry would wash up and go running along the dirt roads for exercise before returning home for dinner. Or he would head down to the high school field and run around for two hours – in his work clothes. "He sure used up some towels, I'll tell you that," she says.

Bricklaying was serious business, especially in temperatures that often exceeded 100 degrees, with humidity as unforgiving as Ezel Wickes. Jerry and his brothers Joe, Tom, Jimmy, and James had a system that depended on rhythm, timing, and precision. Two of them, usually Joe and Jimmy, would toss the bricks from ground level, sliding them expertly from a slick hod – a wooden trough with a long handle used for carrying bricks and mortar – to a third brother up above. The brick-catcher would then apply cement and hand off to Joe Nathan and either Tom or James for the actual laying of the bricks. Jerry was the son who helped his father with the greatest frequency, and when it was his turn to catch, the precious hands that would become the keys to his livelihood took a brutal beating. Journalists have long theorized that this is how Rice developed his hand-eye coordination; he believes it simply enhanced his appreciation for the fruits of labor.

"I think it just taught me hard work," he says. "My father was very demanding, and it was a challenge to keep everything running smoothly. We had to lay a certain number of bricks every day, so he'd really push everybody hard, no matter how sweaty we got. For me, it was a matter of pride. I still look back on those days, because I

Facing page: *Rice ran miles on the dirt roads near his home, establishing a lifelong passion for conditioning.*
Above: *B. L. Moor High's most famous graduate.*

23

remember thinking how this was not something I wanted to be doing for the rest of my life. But at that time it was good to me, because it put money into my pocket and taught me to be able to support myself. I might pull in $300 a week, which back then was pretty good money. I would give money to my mother for food, and I could also go out and get some things for myself."

Invariably, Jerry spent his money on clothes. As shy as he was around his classmates, especially girls, he nonetheless dressed to impress. When his mother, sisters, or niece weren't available to iron his outfit, Jerry would do it himself. If he wore jeans, they had to be clean and starched. "Oh, gracious, if he didn't have but $50, he'd spend that last $50 on a pair of pants to go with a shirt," Eddie B. says. "He loved to look in the mirror. And he always looked just right."

Well, not always. When Rice was in high school, he sometimes would show up in public with blond hair. Was Rice the early incarnation of Dennis Rodman? Was he emulating the look of Golden Richards, one of the Dallas Cowboy receivers he idolized? Was the shy kid with the penchant for natty attire going punk?

No, no, and no. The explanation was far more benign. In order to hang out with his friends on Friday and Saturday nights in the tiny town of Crawford, Rice, who lived several miles away on a stretch of farmland, had to walk up to the dirt roads near his parents' property and thumb a ride. This wasn't exactly a hitchhiker's mecca. Rice couldn't be picky about transportation. Sometimes, he had to get in the cab of a pickup truck. He'd be all duded up and ready to go, his clothes ironed meticulously, his hair combed perfectly. Then the truck would go racing down the dirt roads that led to town, and Rice would get doused with so much dust, his hair would actually appear blond by the time he reached his destination. He might have looked a little freaky at times, but Rice's teenaged entertainment was as wholesome as Richie Cunningham's in *Happy Days*. He and his friends would listen to music, shoot pool, flirt with girls, and cruise around in cars. "I think I had an excellent childhood," Rice says. "Not growing up in the city, that gave me an opportunity to stay away from a lot of bad things. In the city you had drugs and so many things happening around you, so you could get sidetracked a little bit."

But if Rice was a country boy at heart, he still tried to dress like a city slicker – and his obsession with neatness carried over to football. Rather than risking an unkempt uniform, Rice regularly would take his jersey and football pants home and wash them himself. "I felt you had to look good to feel good about yourself, and then you could play well," he says. "I still feel that way today." More than 15,000 receiving yards later, no one is questioning Rice's theory.

It took an uncanny combination of several fortuitous forces to enable Rice to buy his parents a 3,800-square-foot home in Starkville, Mississippi – to realize that childhood dream that he and his older brother Tom had held as long as either one of them could remember. What it took was an innovative coach with a keen eye for raw talent and an audacious offensive scheme; a hard-working quarterback with an arm of gold; Rice's unabashed self-promotion in the presence of NFL scouts; and a certain white-haired wizard who happened to pick up the TV remote control in his Houston hotel room at the perfect time.

> *"He doesn't seem like he has changed any. I think he's the same old Jerry."*
>
> **Eddie B. Rice**

Facing page: *Source of pride: The heart of the Rice family, Jerry's mother, Eddie B.*

Tom had the first crack at payback. He earned a football scholarship to Jackson State, where he played outside linebacker. Jerry remembers the thrill of traveling with his parents from Crawford down to Jackson and watching Tom perform in a jam-packed stadium.

Tom figured if he could get drafted by an NFL team, he'd use his signing bonus to build Joe and Eddie B. a new home. But Jackson State was a Division I-AA school and Tom wasn't quite good enough to make it as a pro. He went undrafted, and his NFL dream was over. Jerry, the second-youngest brother, would have to be the one.

The first step was getting out of Crawford, and that was no small feat. As a high school senior, Jerry drew interest from about 40 colleges, but no one was pounding on his door. Mississippi State was only 20 miles away, and Rice, an All-State end and defensive back in high school, didn't even get a phone call from the Southeastern Conference school. One reason was that his high school team didn't throw much, and when it did, Rice sometimes had to do the throwing. "He played so many positions," recalls Archie "Gunslinger" Cooley, now the assistant coach at Texas Southern University. "Receiver, defensive back, running back, quarterback. Wherever they needed help, they put him in that spot."

Cooley, then the coach at Mississippi Valley State, was the only one who took the time to assess Rice's potential firsthand. Cooley had heard about Rice through his extensive network of black high school coaches, and when he showed up to scout the lanky teenager in Crawford, Rice was so impressed he accepted a scholarship to the little-known Division I-AA school. "No one else came to see me in person," explains Rice, who also was attracted to Cooley's pass-happy offense. Tom Rice, in fact, urged Jerry to go there for that very reason.

Despite his obvious athletic gifts, Rice was hardly a bona fide pro prospect when he arrived in 1981 in Itta Bena, Mississippi – hometown of legendary bluesman B.B. King – at the start of his freshman year. This wasn't Notre Dame or Alabama. Mississippi Valley State had 2,500 students. The town had one stoplight. And Cooley had an offense that never, ever slowed down.

Cooley deployed the Delta Devils in a no-huddle, four-receiver set in which they threw the ball up to 90 percent of the time, which often meant 50 or 60 passes in a game. Rice instantly caught his coach's eye. "The first week of practice, I knew Jerry was a special athlete, because his work ethic was so great," Cooley says. "He was the first one on the practice field, and he'd stay after practice. I attribute his work habits to his father, who worked as a bricklayer in the sun all day and taught Jerry the value of an honest day's work. After that, work wasn't anything to him."

Rice's workplace was far from luxurious. Mississippi Valley State's stadium held 10,500 people, and the practice field contained about 10 times that many mosquitoes. "You'd try to practice and there would be mosquitoes all over you," Rice remembers. "We would go out and buy Off and spray it all over ourselves, but that would only work for a time. Your white pants would be covered with mosquitoes and you still had to stay focused.

"And we didn't have much grass, either – after practicing on that field so much, it would turn to dirt. We'd practice three times a day during the summer, and that grass went away pretty quick."

During his freshman season, Rice's teammates gave

Facing page: *Even in college, trying to cover Rice one-on-one was a futile proposition.*
Above: *From the start, Rice wowed Mississippi Valley State coach Archie Cooley with his work ethic.*

him the nickname "World" – because he could catch anything in the world, they reasoned. Back then, Cooley hadn't completely committed the Delta Devils to the four-receiver set. But in Rice's sophomore season Willie Totten, who had been redshirted the previous year, became the starting quarterback. Finally, the Gunslinger had the perfect person to direct his offense. Totten joined Rice in pre- and post-practice workouts, and the two developed a connection that was downright scary. The offense became known as the Satellite Express, because there were so many airborne objects. Most of the time, Cooley ran a Stack-4 attack that baffled the Delta Devils' Southwestern Athletic Conference foes. The formation featured receivers on each side of the line of scrimmage, with two other receivers stacked directly behind them. Cooley recalls a 1984 game against Southern University in which the Devils went to the Stack-4 after trailing 36-6 at halftime: "We came back to beat them 63-45. Jerry threw three touchdown passes and caught three touchdowns in the second half. We put him in at tailback and tossed backwards passes to him, and he'd throw or run. We put him at fullback and ran him out so a linebacker was on him. We put him anywhere we could to get that ball to him. They hadn't seen the Stack-4 and didn't know how to cover it."

In Rice's sophomore season, he caught 66 passes for 1,133 yards and seven touchdowns. Still, a pro career seemed little more than a fantasy. An electronics major, Rice figured he'd end up as a TV repairman or auto mechanic. "I was good with my hands," he recalls, "so I wanted to go into something like electronics. I could always fix things – if something was broken, I could look

at it and somehow mess around with it and get it to work. I'd fix toasters, radios, television sets, anything that plugged in."

But as the numbers piled up, Rice was forced to take his dream of a pro career more seriously. In a game against Southern during his junior season, Rice caught 24 passes, an all-division record. "He was dead at the end of that game," Cooley recalls. "It was something to see. They kept hammering him after every catch, and he kept getting up." Another highlight that season came when the Delta Devils faced favored Tennessee State. Knowing that opposing defensive backs would try to punish Rice, Cooley had his star receiver, who wore no. 88, switch jerseys with another player, Ron Hill, who wore no. 45. Impersonating Hill meant running routes from an unfamiliar position, but it also meant single coverage for Rice, who scored two touchdowns before Tennessee State had any idea what was happening. He had three touchdowns by halftime, then took the field for the second half wearing no. 88, further confusing the opposition. Mississippi Valley State pulled off a 51-38 upset victory.

By the time he was through, Rice would set 18 Division I-AA records, finishing with a staggering career total of 4,693 receiving yards. In 1984, his senior season, Rice pulled down 112 receptions for 1,845 yards and 28 touchdowns. One game against Kentucky State, Rice caught 12 passes and scored three touchdowns – in the *first quarter*. He finished the game with 17 receptions for 294 yards and five touchdowns, and the Delta Devils won, 86-0. They also won games by scores of 83-11 and 77-15. In that amazing season, Mississippi Valley State averaged 55 points and more than 600 yards per game.

Facing page: The big hands that once caught bricks now gathered footballs at a record rate. **Above:** *Armed and dangerous: Quarterback Willie Totten and Rice were a dynamic duo for the Delta Devils.* **Following pages:** *The grass often disappeared from the Delta Devils' practice field, but the mosquitoes never went away.*

With Totten weakened by the flu, the Delta Devils were bounced from the playoffs by Louisiana Tech by a 66-19 score. Earlier in the week, when it looked like Totten would not be able to play, Rice had taken snaps in practice as the first-string quarterback.

Rice was turning into a hot commodity off the field as well. The shy kid who barely said more than "Yes, sir," to Coach Cooley upon his arrival in Itta Bena was now the big man on campus. "The more touchdowns he scored, the more confidence he developed, and the girls got interested," Cooley says.

The girl who drew the greatest interest from Jerry didn't go to Mississippi Valley State – and she wasn't particularly wowed by his status or the attention that went with it. Jackie Mitchell was a senior on a high school field trip that took her to Itta Bena for a basketball game on campus. Her good looks attracted plenty of oohs and aahs from the young men in the bleachers, while most of the young ladies in attendance were focused on Jerry.

"There were so many guys trying to get next to her and talk to her, and I was sitting a couple of bleachers up," Jerry recalls. "Everybody was coming over and, as we called it, trying to put their bid in. I was sitting there just watching everything, and someone brought me over and introduced us."

The attraction was mutual. Unfortunately, at first it was a negative attraction.

"When we met," Jerry says, "we didn't see eye-to-eye. We started talking but we didn't hit it off at first. I don't know why. I guess we just disagreed. And we really got into an argument. It was not nice at all."

It began with a misunderstanding. Jackie's friends had been making a big commotion over Jerry Rice, but she had no idea who he was. She might have been the only person in the gym that day unaware of Rice's small-school football stardom. "We were sitting there talking," Jackie says, "and every girl in the Coliseum was trying to get him to look over." The ogling didn't bother Jerry, but Jackie was not amused.

"I don't know if this is a good idea," she told him. "Either sit here and focus on me, or go talk to them."

"You're spoiled," Jerry shot back. "You like having things your way, don't you?"

The conversation stayed chilly, but as it wound down, Jerry asked Jackie for her phone number and told her he would call her at noon the next day. He phoned at 12 on the nose. She invited him to visit her at her family's Greenville, Mississippi home, and they spent the day together. The manners he had been taught by his parents served him well.

With one simple gesture, Rice won over his future mother-in-law, Gloria.

"He was the perfect gentleman," Jackie says. "My mom was very particular about the guys I dated, and

Facing page: *Rice was a hot commodity at Mississippi Valley State, but it took more than flashy moves to win over Jackie, his future wife.*

when he met her the first thing he did was he stood up to shake her hand. Most guys that age just didn't do that. She thought that was so impressive."

Oddly enough, it was Rice's *lack* of decorum that won over the NFL scouts who stopped by to check out the fireworks in Itta Bena. The school didn't have sophisticated video equipment, and when scouts would come to the football office to view tapes of the Delta Devils, Rice invariably would stop by to enhance their viewing experience. Most college players have little or no contact with scouts, but as a small-school standout, Rice figured it was up to him to inform them of his greatness. So he would sit in on their film sessions and offer a running narration.

"Watch that move," he'd shout. "Run that back, run that back. Right there, this is my greatest move."

Says Cooley: "Jerry wanted to play this game real bad, so he would go in there and rah-rah himself and pat himself on the back. The scouts would be on the floor laughing. Sometimes I knew he was worrying them, because they had a job to do. But he developed a relationship with the scouts, and that

really helped. They could attach a face to the name when they filed their evaluations. Plus, he was a 'Yes, sir' person, and they loved that."

Scouts also loved Rice's performance in the Blue-Gray game following his senior season. In an All-Star game featuring mostly Division I competition, Rice was named the Most Valuable Player. But the skepticism persisted, especially after he staged a workout attended by scouts from several NFL teams and was timed at a relatively mundane 4.6 seconds in the 40-yard-dash.

One thing must be understood about Jerry Rice's speed: He is not stopwatch-fast, but in a football uniform and pads, with the ball in the air and a defender on his tail, he's about as swift as they come. Or, to put it better, he's as swift as he needs to be. Though he was caught by defensive backs in his first exhibition game as a rookie, Rice has not been run down from behind since.

To many scouts, however, the stopwatch is God. Fortunately for Rice, the coach of the world champion San Francisco 49ers, future Hall of Famer Bill Walsh, was of a different mind.

"I thought Jerry would be picked in the first five selections in the draft," Walsh says. "But as we talked to our colleagues in the NFL, somehow, some way, he had run a 4.6 40, so he had been downgraded. It was easy for scouts to dismiss Jerry because of his time. Because otherwise, they would have had to project a player from Mississippi Valley State as a major NFL contributor, and that's a tough one to sell to management and coaches. This way, they could deflect the idea by saying, 'Well, it's a small college and he has a slow time.' We had one scout decide that Jerry couldn't play in the NFL – that he wouldn't draft him before the sixth round, that he was a product of the system, whatever he meant by that. Well, that was just bizarre, ridiculous."

Though there were other quality receivers in the draft that year – including two players who would be picked ahead of Rice, Al Toon (Jets) and Eddie Brown (Bengals) – Walsh had been obsessed with Rice since the previous October. The night before the 49ers played the Oilers in the Astrodome, Walsh lay in bed in his Houston hotel room, flipping through the channels as he prepared himself for sleep. He heard an announcer say, "We've got

*Facing page: Cooley locked Rice in a bear hug (above) but let him run free in games, making happy campers out of the Delta Devils (below). **Above:** After a 51-38 victory over Tennessee State in Memphis in1983, Rice and Totten stood tall.*

some highlights you won't believe coming after this," and he dutifully stayed tuned during the commercial break. Then, sure enough, he saw Rice doing things he couldn't believe. There was no. 88 slashing across the screen and dashing into the end zone. The same player went deep for a score, then sliced through coverage, then made a diving grab in the end zone. There were five touchdown catches in all, and Walsh went to bed thinking, "Well, someday we'll play against this guy, because there's not a chance in hell we'll ever have him ourselves."

A few months later, the 49ers were in the worst possible position to draft Rice. That was of their own doing. By sweeping through the league with 18 regular and postseason victories, culminating in a 38-16 Super Bowl shellacking of the Miami Dolphins, the 49ers – who set a league record for most combined wins in the regular season and the playoffs – assured themselves the 28th and last pick of the first round. But come draft time, Walsh was known to engage in more high-stakes trading than Wall Street, and 1985 would be no exception.

"I didn't know how it could ever be done," Walsh says, "but I had a fixation on Jerry from the time I watched those highlights, because he was one player I knew would be great. Typically, we had a history of looking for alternatives as the draft developed – trading up or trading down. But we had just won the Super Bowl, so how could we do anything to get someone like Jerry Rice?"

To pull it off, the 49ers had to gamble. Two days before the draft, general manager John McVay came to Walsh and said, "You know, I might have something in New England." The Patriots had offered their first-round pick (16th overall) and third-round selection for the 49ers' choices in the first, second, and third rounds. Walsh

wanted to see how things shook down on draft day, and the two teams agreed to keep the option open until the midpoint of the first round.

Two days later, when Buffalo picked cornerback Derrick Burroughs with the 14th selection, McVay got on the phone to New England and worked the deal. But the 49ers had to sweat out Kansas City's pick at no. 15 – running back Ethan Horton – before getting their man. Then Walsh smiled broadly and prepared to make an historic choice. Given Rice's obscure collegiate background, the spot at which he was selected and the impact he ultimately had on the franchise, this was arguably the best draft pick in NFL history.

Most people who heard about the pick were surprised. There was outright shock in two places: at Rice's house in Jackson, Mississippi, and at the Cowboys' headquarters in Dallas. The team Rice had grown up idolizing was all geared up, they would later say, to take him with the 17th selection, but the 49ers beat them to the punch. "Well you always hear that," Walsh says. "Teams said that about Joe Montana, too: 'Gee, we were right there.' "

Sitting in his brother's living room, Rice was stunned. Many teams had kept in regular contact with him in the weeks leading up to the draft, and he expected to go to either the Cowboys, Green Bay Packers, San Diego Chargers, or Indianapolis Colts. The 49ers weren't even in the realm of possibility. "When they picked me, it was like a sigh of relief," Rice says. Then reality set in. "Oh my God," Rice thought, "I'm going to San Francisco, a big city where I've never been, the team that just won the Super Bowl."

And then came an even more outrageous realization: *I'm going to play with Joe Montana!*

Above: *When Walsh and the 49ers snagged Rice on draft day with the 16th overall selection, it was arguably the best NFL pick of all time.*
Facing page: *Rice left small-college stardom for a job in the big city – and the promise of playing with Joe Montana.*

The Montana Years (1985 - 1990)

The first time they met, Jerry Rice was nervous. It was the spring of 1985 – the 49ers were beginning a post-draft mini-camp for rookies and veterans. Here was Rice, the team's prized

Facing page: *For six seasons, the 49ers were blessed with a harmonic convergence of two of the game's all-time greats: Joe Montana and Jerry Rice.* **Above:** *NFL trophy awarded to Rice, Super Bowl XXIII MVP, containing a miniature of the Vince Lombardi Trophy.*

rookie, about to shake the hand of Joe Montana, two-time Super Bowl MVP and worldwide sporting hero. "I had watched him on television, I had seen him make so many incredible plays and pull out so many last-minute victories," Rice says. "I was a little bit in awe."

It was the rest of the NFL that had reason to be nervous. In one of those harmonic convergences of athletic immortality, the greatest quarterback of all time would spend the next six seasons throwing to the greatest receiver of all time. Either player would have been a superstar without the other. Together, they ascended to a plane that had not previously existed. Montana and Rice were the football equivalent of Ruth and Gehrig, or Magic and Kareem – or, if you prefer, Lennon and McCartney.

Meeting the quarterback turned out to be a mellow interaction. "I thought a guy of his status would be conceited, not give me the time of day," Rice remembers. "But it was the opposite. He was very relaxed and willing to talk to you and help you out in any way possible."

By the end of the first mini-camp practice, everyone was talking about Rice. The first person to take notice of Rice's amazing skill level was Dwight Clark, the 49ers' All-Pro receiver. Clark was the man who, in the 1981 NFC Championship game, soared up in the back of the north end zone at Candlestick Park to make The Catch, the play that defeated the Dallas Cowboys and launched a dynasty. When Clark came off the field after Rice's practice debut, he ran over to Walsh, pointed at the rookie and said, "What is THAT?"

"He couldn't believe it," Walsh says. "First workout, and we were saying, 'What do we have here?' Jerry was

so much further ahead than most people you draft, so we knew right away he would play."

"He was raw," says Clark, now the 49ers' vice president and director of football operations, "but he just had this ability to get his hands on the ball, no matter where he was and no matter who was covering him."

The first people who tried to cover Rice were the best defensive backs in the business. All four members of the 49ers' secondary – cornerbacks Ronnie Lott and Eric Wright, and safeties Carlton Williamson and Dwight Hicks – had played in the Pro Bowl following the 1984 season, the first and only time that has happened. And yet when Rice arrived, they flailed around like helpless journeymen.

"None of these guys would ever admit this, particularly Ronnie and Eric, but I got the distinct impression that he broke them," says 49ers head coach George Seifert, who was the defensive coordinator at the time. "In other words, guys have a certain confidence and arrogance about them that they have to have in order to play those positions, and he ran by all of them so many times in practice that it was kind of like he demoralized them. Eventually, as they got a feel for him, it got better. But initially there was a week or so where I could almost see it in their eyes."

Rice might not have revealed it then, but he, too, was unnerved. The reserved kid from Mississippi was overwhelmed by the fast pace of his new lifestyle: the size and sophistication of San Francisco, the big rookie contract, the complexity of Walsh's playbook. When he flew in from Mississippi after being drafted – only the second time he'd been on an airplane – Rice was astounded to find a horde of mini-cams and reporters in

Above: *From the start of training camp in 1985, All-Pro receiver Dwight Clark (87) took Rice under his wing.*
Facing page: *Rice responded to the challenges of his first NFL season with dedication and determination.*

"His first year, he kept his mouth shut and just listened. Most rookies try to come

in like they know it all and try to show the veterans how cool they are.

Jerry didn't come in and boast that he was the best receiver in the league.

He just kept his mouth shut and kept working hard."

his face when he arrived at the airport. "I was just scared to step off the plane," Rice says. "There were so many people running at me from so many different directions. I didn't know how to carry myself. I did my best to deal with it, but it made me feel uncomfortable. I'm coming to this big city and there's nobody that I know. I wanted to turn around and go back on the plane, go back home."

Jackie, his future wife (they would marry on September 8, 1987), was still a pre-med student at the University of Southern Mississippi. During their daily telephone conversations, Jerry told her he was struggling with life in the fast lane. "Coming from a small town and a small college, it was a bit overwhelming for him," she says. "And there were so many expectations put on him."

All of these forces combined to cause Rice to struggle in the one area he'd always taken for granted: catching the ball. As amazing as it seems now, at the beginning of his career Rice was known more for the passes he dropped than the ones he caught. Reporters began referring to him as a potential bust. Teammates called him "Butterfingers," sometimes to his face. Even Montana, the man they called Joe Cool, cast chilly glares in Rice's direction after some of his perfectly thrown passes ricocheted off the receiver's hands.

"It was brutal," Rice says. "I had to do a lot of soul-searching. Joe's a very patient guy, but when he's putting the ball right there on the money he feels like you should catch the football, and I kept dropping it. He didn't say it, but you could tell that he was starting to have doubts. And so were my teammates. I'd walk through the locker room and hear little whispers. You might walk over and all of a sudden the conversation is a little dry, a little stale, and you know something's wrong. You can feel it. And that's a very uncomfortable predicament to be in, because I think the most important thing is to have the support of your teammates, and they're only gonna stick with you for so long if things are not going right."

Says Montana: "You could just tell he was trying too hard. You knew it was just a matter of time. A lot of rookies get in there and they just want to make a play. You want to do everything possible to make everyone think you're worthy of being a no. 1 pick; I know I did, and I was a third-rounder. You try so hard and when you screw up, you think everybody's looking at you, thinking how you don't belong – even if they're not."

No one knows exactly how many footballs Rice actually dropped that first season. One reporter counted 11 in Rice's first 11 games. Another said Rice had 10 drops halfway through the season. Walsh had moved Rice into the starting lineup ahead of veteran Freddie Solomon early in the season, but after Rice began treating the ball like toxic waste, Solomon got his job back in week 10.

The next Sunday the 49ers hosted Kansas City at Candlestick Park, and Rice's stock dropped to its all-time low. In the first half, Montana threw him two passes, a 30-yarder downfield and a 10-yarder up the middle. Twice, Rice was wide open. Both balls clanged off his hands. The hometown fans booed loudly on both occasions and did the same as Rice headed to the locker room at the end of the first half. When Frisbee-catching dogs took the field at halftime, one fan yelled, "Rice, take note." In the locker room, Rice began sobbing and had to be consoled by several teammates and Walsh.

Above: *Rice dresses for his first NFL regular-season game, a 28-21 defeat at Minnesota.* **Facing page:** *The spawning of a legend: Rice soars to make his first professional reception during an exhibition victory over the Raiders at the L.A. Coliseum.*

"Some of the insensitive fans at Candlestick – and this is typical of any city – used to boo Jerry," Walsh says. "They wanted their Freddie Solomon in there, and here was this new one from Mississippi Valley State – 'What are you doing with him?' He came in at halftime, and he was far more affected by it than I expected. I wasn't alerted to it until just before we went out for the second half: he had broken down and was very emotional and very hurt."

Says Rice: "Oh man, there were many games where I just went in and cried. I cried because I had always been able to catch a football and make a play, and now I was dropping footballs and I just couldn't pinpoint what was going on. I had never been booed before, and that was really hard. Bill and the coaches just kept telling me, 'Just keep working hard.' In a situation like that, they could've just slammed the door on me and said, 'OK, bad draft choice, let's get rid of him.' But I guess Bill saw something in me and stuck with me. He can see something in a football player that no one else can see."

The 49ers were in the process of winning that game against Kansas City by a 31-3 score, but Rice's travails continued. With five minutes remaining, Walsh instructed backup quarterback Matt Cavanaugh to throw the ball to his prized rookie, who had yet to make a catch in the game. Cavanaugh threw a short pass and Rice caught it, dashed eight yards downfield ... and fumbled. Montana, Clark, Roger Craig, and receiver Mike Wilson huddled around Rice and told him to keep his head up. "Hey," Clark offered, "I dropped four passes against Chicago in my rookie year, and two of them were on third down."

Rice remains grateful for the support he received from Clark, and especially from Solomon, who was perhaps the most unlikely tutor imaginable. Rice had been brought in to take Solomon's job, yet Solomon, who retired after the season, quickly became the rookie's confidante, cheerleader, and mentor. "It really showed a lot of character," Rice says. "It's very hard when you know you're at the end and someone has come in to take your job. But he and Dwight passed the torch on, and I'll pass it on, because it's a tradition. I guess that's why we've had so much success around here."

Two weeks after the Kansas City game, the 49ers played at Washington, and Rice, for the second time in his career, went an entire game without making a catch.

No one had any inkling that, eight days later, Rice would leave each and every one of his doubters gaping in amazement. In a Monday Night Football showdown

"When I first came into the league, I just liked to spend time off by myself. I'm able to deal with it better now, but I'm still shy."

Jerry Rice

Facing page: *Plagued by a run of dropped passes, Rice felt like an outsider during the first part of his rookie season.*

with the rival Los Angeles Rams at Candlestick for the NFC Western Division title, a national TV audience saw Rice realize his vast potential in one bold stroke of genius. "I call that my Coming Out Game," Rice says. "I went in really relaxed, and when it was over, I knew I could play professional football."

Rice caught 10 passes for 241 yards, a team record at the time. He caught a 66-yard touchdown pass from Montana and a 52-yarder that set up another score. The 49ers lost 27-20, but Rice gained instant respect. "He made the All-Rookie team in one night," Dwight Clark says. "The frustrations of the first 13 games all disappeared and everything clicked." And in Roger Craig's words, "He shut a lot of people up real quick."

One of those people was a certain Los Angeles Raiders honcho who Bill Walsh coyly refers to as "one of the famous men in the NFL." The 49ers had opened the 1985 exhibition season against the Raiders at the L.A. Coliseum. On one play Rice caught a sideline bomb and appeared to be on his way to an 80-yard touch-down before two of the swiftest L.A. defenders angled over and dragged him down from behind. After the game, Walsh says the Raiders honcho told him, "You see that, there's a lack of speed. You notice our guys caught him."

Walsh's response: "Give me a break." The coach knew that at the end of the run Rice had tightened up, shortening his stride and leaning his body back. It was a simple error to rectify, and Rice was obviously paying attention during the following day's film session: Hundreds of players have since tried, but no one else has been able to chase him down.

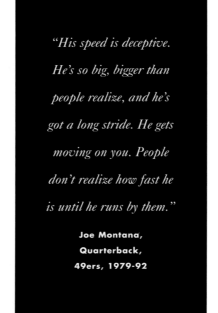

"His speed is deceptive. He's so big, bigger than people realize, and he's got a long stride. He gets moving on you. People don't realize how fast he is until he runs by them."

Joe Montana, Quarterback, 49ers, 1979-92

The one time Rice failed to complete a breakaway dash to the end zone was on a play that would haunt him for two years. On the heels of a remarkable second season for which he was honored as NFL Player of the Year by *Sports Illustrated*, Rice went from hero to zero in 2.4 seconds. Less than three minutes into a first-round playoff game against the Giants, Rice caught a quick slant from Montana and broke free into the open field. He was going all the way, but got careless. Held too close to his thigh, the ball came loose in mid-stride, rolling all the way into the end zone for a touchback. The 49ers ended up losing the game, 49-3. In keeping with his nature, Rice shouldered the blame.

"I can still see that ball just rolling along the ground," he says. "Never bouncing, just rolling sideways on the turf. That play really changed the momentum of the game, and it taught me in a situation like that to secure the football and don't relax until you get across that goal line."

In 1987, Rice set what may be the most astounding single-season record in NFL history: 22 touchdown receptions, four more than previous record holder Mark Clayton caught for the Miami Dolphins in 1984. Clayton's mark had been achieved in a full 16-game season. Rice, his duty restricted by the 1987 players' strike, compiled his total in just 12 games. He was voted the league's MVP, a rarity for a receiver. He led the league in scoring, the first receiver to do so since Elroy "Crazy Legs" Hirsch in 1951. He extended a streak of consecutive games with at least one touchdown catch to a league-record 13.

There was no more doubt about Rice – he was a bona fide NFL star, with his own nickname: "Flash 80."

Facing page: *The offensive heart and soul of the Super Bowl 49ers: (left to right) Joe Montana, Jerry Rice, and Roger Craig.*

He celebrated touchdown catches by doing a funky routine dubbed the "Cabbage Patch Dance." He drove fancy cars with personalized license plates. He drew attention to himself with his immaculate appearance, the stylishly displayed towel hanging from his uniform and his poofy hairdo. Teammates called him "Fifi," and when he showed up for training camp in 1987 with a particularly elevated head of hair, he earned the nickname "6-7" – as in 6-2, with five inches of hair.

The image was fun, but there was one slight problem: it had nothing to do with the real Jerry Rice. As flashy as he could appear on the field, Rice's success had been forged by hard work and intense passion for his craft. But in the early part of his career, he seemed to be composed of more style than substance.

"He was young," Jackie says. "He was just having a good time, being young and doing something to express himself. But everyone focused on the way he dressed and on his hair. There are so many other interesting things about him."

Walsh says Rice felt a need to draw attention to himself because the 49ers' other stars – Montana, Craig, Lott, and Clark among them – soaked up so much of the spotlight. "He almost felt that he was going to be upstaged," Walsh says. "There's so much posturing that goes on that, unfortunately, has been glorified by television, and guys almost feel bound to do that or are cajoled to by their contemporaries."

"That was me trying to fit in," Rice says. "There was a lot of that going on, and you're always looking for something different, so people can relate to you. I was doing that little dance, and after awhile I said, 'Jerry, what are you doing? Just be yourself. You don't have to do anything crazy like that. Just go out there and have fun.' "

In time, Montana's understated elegance began to rub off on Rice, who in later years would come to symbolize the essence of dignity in the NFL. And really, how could Rice not be affected by Montana? The two didn't pal around much off the field, but in the heat of battle, they shared a cosmic connection that transcended the madness and violence around them. Rice once said, "I know exactly what Joe is thinking at all times. When I get up to the line of scrimmage, I know exactly when the ball will be coming."

Because of Rice's dogged determination and willingness to fight desperately for the ball, Montana viewed him as a potential target on any pass play. "You just knew if there was anyone on the field working to get open, it was Jerry," Montana says. "Even if the coverage was tight, you knew he would be working hard and you knew that if you stuck it in there, you'd have a pretty good chance of completing it. In tight situations, when the game was close, there were times I'd throw balls to him that I might not throw to anyone else."

In addition to their obvious talents, Montana and Rice shared a gnawing fear of failure, as if their respective identities were threatened by anything less than perfection. Because of this, the 49ers were never, ever out of a game. In the second game of the 1987 season, at Cincinnati's Riverfront Stadium, San Francisco trailed the Bengals, 26-20, with six seconds remaining. Cincinnati had the ball in its own territory on fourth down and two yards to go. A punt almost certainly would have ended the game, but Bengals coach Sam Wyche, in

Above: *Rice's funky hairdo led teammates to call him "Fifi." Says receiving mate John Taylor: "He didn't like that too much."*
Facing page: *Despite being sidelined for four games due to the players' strike, Rice caught a league-record 22 touchdown passes in 1987.*

a truly bizarre decision, ran a sweep to the left. The 49ers stopped Cincinnati halfback James Brooks at the 25-yard-line with two seconds remaining, and the clock stopped with the change of possession.

Montana and Rice came bouncing back onto the field like a couple of kids on the last day at school. Needing a Hail Mary pass, the 49ers lined up three receivers to the left and Rice to the right. The Bengals put cornerback Eric Thomas in man-to-man coverage on Rice, which is sort of like leaving a single prison guard to watch over Hannibal Lecter. "Anytime you have one-on-one coverage on Jerry, I'll take my chances," Montana says. "I just lined up over center and tried not to stare over there." Montana lofted the ball to the corner of the end zone and Rice soared above Thomas for the game-winning catch. It was immediately dubbed the 49ers' "Hail Jerry" play.

"We didn't really have time to think about it because we ran on the field so fast," Rice recalls. "I went up to catch the ball, and everyone was looking around in amazement. Bill [Walsh] was skipping off the field. I think [team owner] Eddie DeBartolo missed it – he had gone to the locker room because he was so pissed off, and he was getting ready to light into us."

The next September at Giants Stadium, Montana and Rice provided an even more fantastic finish. The 49ers trailed the Giants, 17-13, with 42 seconds remaining. Montana took the snap from his own 22-yard-line and hummed a medium-range pass down the sidelines. "They were in a soft, two-deep zone, and we were just trying to get down the field," Montana says. "I threw the ball in the seam, and the rest was all Jerry." The ball looked unreachable, but Rice got there. Cornerback Mark Collins and safety Kenny Hill each arrived a half-second later and collided; Rice sprinted down the sidelines for the winning touchdown.

"I'll never forget that environment," Rice says. "What a hostile crowd! As I ran to the end zone, the New York fans were so quiet. That really felt good. When I go back and look at some of those old tapes, I'm not looking at the catch, I'm looking at the reaction – of the guys on the sidelines, and of the fans, because that's something you never get a chance to see during the game."

The 78-yard scoring play was of much importance to the 49ers, who went on to capture their third Super Bowl that season. But to future head coach George Seifert, then the 49ers' defensive coordinator, it took on an even greater significance. "I've got a film that I keep in my office that I show to the players every year," he says. "We played the Giants back there in the 1986 playoffs and [Rice] took some ungodly cheap shots from their safety. He'd be down on one knee, and the play would be over, and the guy would come in and spear him or elbow him. These were the most ruthless cheap shots I've ever seen.

"I've never seen a player accepted and assimilated so smoothly and so quickly as Jerry, on any team."

Bill Walsh,
Hall of Fame Coach

Facing page: *It took four seasons for Rice to become a Super Bowl champion, but he always carried himself like one.*
Following pages: *By 1987, it wasn't too much to say that Rice was the NFL's foremost offensive weapon.*

And he never got flagged. So the tape has those clips, and then it has the clip of Jerry's game-winning catch down the sidelines two years later. The same safety is coming over to make the play, and Jerry brushes right by him and goes all the way. My point was, you've got to maintain your cool. Instead of jumping up and fighting with him and both of you getting thrown out of the game, it hurts the other player more if you beat him as a player."

Rice's toughness has always been obscured by his more obvious attributes, but players around the NFL know him to be a fierce competitor who does not shy away from contact. "A lot of people don't believe this, but Jerry is not a guy you're gonna go out and intimidate," says All-Pro cornerback Eric Davis, a 49er from 1990 to 1995 who now plays for Carolina. "He wouldn't have been able to accomplish the things he had if he couldn't take a hit. Most offensive players tend to get a little gun shy, but he's not afraid of the contact. He's a football player."

Yet after three NFL seasons, Rice was a football player who had yet to win a playoff game. In three post-season appearances from 1985 to 1987, all convincing defeats, Rice had totaled a mere 10 catches for 121 yards and no touchdowns. There were even people questioning his heart. But during a three-week stretch that began on New Year's Day, 1989, and ended with a Super Bowl MVP trophy, Rice answered his critics with enough big-game brilliance to last a lifetime.

On January 1, 1989, the Minnesota Vikings came to Candlestick Park for a divisional playoff game. The previous year, the Vikings had contained Rice, who had a sprained ankle, and scored a stunning 36-24 victory over the 49ers. This time, Rice left them no opening for a repeat performance. He caught three first-half touchdown passes, tying an NFL single-game postseason record, as the 49ers cruised to a 34-9 victory.

The next week the 49ers traveled to Chicago, where the favored Bears, and some of the coldest weather in NFL playoff history, loomed. Most experts figured the frigid temperatures, which approached 50 degrees below zero when the wind-chill factor was considered, would work against San Francisco and its vaunted passing game in the NFC Championship game. To show that they would not be psyched out, a group of 49ers, Rice included, came out for pregame warm-ups wearing short sleeves. "I was all pumped up," Rice says. "I was thinking, 'I don't care, I can do whatever I want to out here today.' So I ran out there in my short sleeves, and I almost froze to death. I ran back into the locker room and put on long sleeves."

The Bears should have bolted the locker room door, because once Rice took the field, they were done. In the first quarter, Rice ran a 20-yard pattern and broke off to the sidelines, where he came back to meet a hard-thrown pass from Montana. Rice caught the ball, and two Chicago defensive backs closed in for the tackle. Then Rice made a move that would have frozen any defender under any conditions: he stepped toward the would-be tacklers and just as quickly reversed his ground. The two players watched helplessly as Rice broke free and dashed 61 yards for a touchdown. "I don't think anyone thought I could make a cut like that because the ground was all frozen," Rice says. Later in the first half, Rice made another great move after a short catch and turned it into a 27-yard scoring play, and the 49ers won, 28-3.

Facing page: *Rice learned early on that after getting knocked down, the sweetest form of revenge was to race to the end zone.*
Above: *Even in frigid Chicago, with a wind-chill factor of close to 50-below during the 1988 NFC Championship game, Rice had the hot hands.*

55

"You never see him stumble or fall or stretch out or lay out. He has that ability to run underneath the ball and catch it on a dead run, dead stride, and never slow down ... When he catches it he's going full speed."

Dan Reeves, Head Coach, New York Giants

For the third time in the decade San Francisco had reached the Super Bowl, this time, on January 22, 1989, against the Cincinnati Bengals at Miami's Joe Robbie Stadium. Despite race riots in Overtown, a low-income area of Miami, Rice was able to focus intensely on the game plan for Super Bowl XXIII. As usual, he spent the day before the game visualizing plays, running through different scenarios in his mind. "Oh boy, I remember the night before the game," he says. "I couldn't sleep. I was up pacing around at 4 a.m., just playing the game over and over in my head. I knew exactly what to expect."

This is what the 49ers got from Rice: 11 receptions for a Super Bowl record 215 yards and an amazing touchdown in which Rice, while falling out of bounds, managed to extend his arm and barely scrape the football over the end-zone pylon. "We had some plays called for him, but there were other plays where he just got open," Montana says. "On one play, he took off down the field, improvised on a route and put up his hand. In that type of game, you wouldn't normally throw the ball in a situation like that, but he made it happen."

Rice caught three passes for 51 yards on the classic, game-winning drive, which the 49ers began on their own eight-yard-line with 3:10 remaining.

"The second we took the field for the final drive, I knew we had the game won," Rice recalls. "Because we had done that drill so many, many times. Whenever it's crunch time, that team had the tendency to respond. Joe came in the huddle, and no one said anything. We were on grass, and I think if a pin had dropped, you would have heard that pin. The focus was there. We started moving the ball downfield. We knew that every play was crucial. Joe was very relaxed, because I think he knew.

He knew that all he had to do was not throw an interception, and other guys would make the plays.

"John Taylor came up with the big catch. I was on the far right side and John was on the left. I think everybody knew the ball was coming my way. I had to come across in motion, and the defense shifted that direction and John had his guy one-on-one. When Joe released that ball I knew John would make the catch." Taylor cradled a picturesque 10-yard pass from Montana in the back of the end zone with 34 seconds remaining, completing the most exciting finish in Super Bowl history and stamping the 49ers, who won by a 20-16 score, as the undisputed Team of the Decade.

Under normal circumstances, Rice, named the Super Bowl MVP, would have been the game's biggest story for days afterward. But Montana had added an amazing chapter to his fairy-tale career, Taylor had made the big catch, and Bill Walsh was in the process of deciding whether to step down as the 49ers' coach. A few days after the game, Walsh resigned, and Seifert was named his successor. Rice, meanwhile, was surprised by the lack of recognition and endorsement opportunities he had received. Two days after the game, he gave an on-camera interview to a San Francisco television reporter and complained about it. Rice said it would have been different had Montana or Dwight Clark been the MVP. Asked if he was implying that racism might be involved, Rice replied, "Yeah, I would say so." The comments generated a major controversy and were criticized by many journalists, who noted that it was a media panel that overwhelmingly picked Rice over Montana as the game's MVP. People called him self-serving and greedy.

Rice still believes he was justified in speaking out, but that he failed to get his point across.

"If I could, I'm not gonna say take it back but reword it, I would," Rice says. "Because people thought it was only about endorsements. It was never about the endorsements. The respect is the most important thing, and that's the only thing I wanted. I felt like I went out there and I exemplified leadership and character and made great plays and I really deserved the respect, and I just didn't get it."

The following January, Rice got to experience what Montana had the previous year: an amazing Super Bowl performance with no MVP trophy to show for it. After romping through the 1989 regular season with a 14-2 record and punishing two playoff opponents, the 49ers earned a Super Bowl XXIV showdown with the Denver Broncos on January 28, 1990. In the days before the game, Denver's defensive backs made a big deal about stopping Rice, saying their aggressive safeties, Dennis Smith and Steve Atwater, would be looming in the secondary, waiting to deliver punishing hits. Not only were the Broncos underestimating Rice's toughness, they were providing added incentive to one of the world's most motivated men.

"I remember all of those remarks," Rice says. "It was like a challenge for me. You had these guys saying, 'I don't think the San Francisco receivers can take a hit.' And I'm like, 'Hey, without a doubt, we have some very physical receivers here.' So that got the blood flowing right there. I was so pumped up going into that game, I couldn't wait for the kickoff. They called us out, and we went to war."

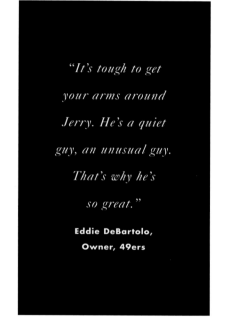

"It's tough to get your arms around Jerry. He's a quiet guy, an unusual guy. That's why he's so great."

Eddie DeBartolo, Owner, 49ers

The game essentially ended with 4:54 gone from the first quarter. From the Denver 20 yard line, Montana dropped back and threw a short pass to Rice, who had run a slant pattern and was in the middle of the field. Atwater had a clear shot at him; this was to be the moment of truth. Atwater raced up and smacked Rice as hard as he could. Rice bounced right off him and cruised into the end zone, leaving Atwater on the ground and the Broncos without a hope. The score was only 6-0, but everyone in the Louisiana Superdome crowd of 72,919 – not to mention the hundreds of millions watching on television around the world – knew it was over. Rice finished with seven receptions for 148 yards and three touchdowns, Montana (22-of-29, 297 yards, five touchdowns) won a record third Super Bowl MVP award, and the 49ers won by a 55-10 score. It was the biggest blowout in Super Bowl history.

"I know fans don't like to see ball games like that where you just blow away the other team completely, but that was the type of game I could really enjoy," Rice says. "Super Bowl XXIII was probably the best game, but in XXIV I had a chance to relax and just take it all in."

The 1990 season was somewhat choppier. There were defensive lapses, and a knee injury to Roger Craig caused the 49ers' running game to struggle. But the team managed to compile another 14-2 regular-season record. At many points during the season, San Francisco was carried by Montana and Rice. Montana won his second consecutive regular-season MVP award, and Rice became the fourth player to catch 100 passes in an NFL season. On one October Sunday in Atlanta, the two legends staged a performance that even by their standards was spectacular.

Facing page: *Pumped up by brash talk from Denver's physical safeties, Rice charged into Super Bowl XXIV and stepped all over the Broncos.*

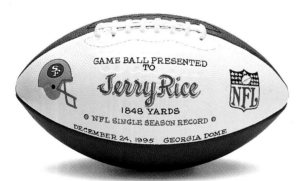

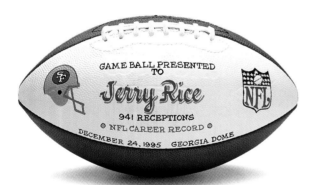

Bound for Canton, Ohio:

Sometime early in the next century

these treasures will be part

of the Jerry Rice display in the

Pro Football Hall of Fame.

Above: *Game balls commemorating career achievements: (top) 14,005 career receiving yards, breaking James Lofton's record on October 29, 1995; (middle) 1,848 single-season yards, set December 24, 1995; (bottom) in the same game, Rice set an NFL record of 941 career receptions, overtaking Art Monk.* **Right:** *The helmet Rice wore when he broke Jim Brown's all-time touchdown record.*

The division-rival Atlanta Falcons were coached by Jerry Glanville, a flamboyant motor-mouth who believed in the blitz and was perhaps the most stubborn man in the history of his profession. All game long, Glanville sent extra pass rushers at Montana and left young cornerback Charles Dimry to cover Rice one-on-one – football's version of cruel and unusual punishment. As Rice says of Dimry: "They just hung him out to dry."

If blitzing Montana is like leaving a fancy car unlocked in a crime-ridden neighborhood, leaving Rice in single coverage is like placing a "Steal Me" sign on the front windshield. Rice burned Dimry for five touchdown receptions, tying an NFL record. He caught 13 passes for 225 yards and surpassed Dwight Clark as the 49ers' career leader in receiving yards. Montana set team records with six touchdown passes and 476 passing yards and needed most of them, too – the 49ers only won by a 45-35 score.

"It's tough duty for anyone to cover Jerry all day long, even when you have help," Montana says. "Anytime you see single-coverage [on Rice], you know your chances are about 95 percent you're gonna get a touchdown."

Rice remembers his amazement at Glanville's insistence on continuing to blitz, even when everyone in Fulton County Stadium was sure it was a horrible idea. "I remember going to the sidelines after catching two touchdowns and hearing some of my teammates say, 'You're gonna catch four or five today,' " Rice says. "Everything was happening so fast. You would think in a situation with them bringing everybody all the time and us picking everything up and scoring touchdowns that eventually they would stop. But they just kept doing it. After I scored the third one I just shook my head – I couldn't believe it was still happening."

It got so that, as he would approach the line of scrimmage and notice the Falcons in the same blitzing formation, Rice would break into a smile and say under his breath: "Come on, snap the ball. Just snap it. They're coming." He caught touchdown no. 4, then no. 5. Sitting in the press box, Atlanta *Journal-Constitution* football writer Len Pasquarelli shook his head and said, "I hope Charles Dimry has good medical records." The poor guy had been burned beyond recognition.

On that spectacular day, it seemed as though Montana and Rice might be able to sustain their magic forever. But fate would not allow it to last beyond the season.

Bill Walsh,
Hall of Fame Coach

Facing page: *By the end of their tenure together, Rice and Montana had developed such a strong chemistry that opponents could not keep up.* **Following pages:** *In 1990, his last full season with Montana, Rice was chosen* Sports Illustrated's *NFL Player of the Year, leading the league in receptions (100) and yardage (1,502).*

The Young Years (1991 - Present)

Jerry Rice was spoiled, and he knew it. For six seasons, he looked up from his routes to find perfect touch passes spiraling over his shoulder and into his outstretched hands.

Facing page: *Rice broke Jim Brown's all-time touchdown record in the 1994 season opener at the Raiders' expense.*
Above: *1994 Mackey Award, presented to Rice by the NFL Players Association as National Football Conference MVP.*

Rice knew where his quarterback would be and in what order and cadence the various receiving options would be assessed. It was like that with Joe Montana, and Rice had no inclination to give up the good life.

But on a cool August night in Seattle in 1991, it became painfully clear something was wrong with Montana's right elbow. San Francisco 49ers doctors, in a hastily arranged press conference following an exhibition game, said there were "minute tears" in Montana's elbow tendons. By October, when Montana underwent major surgery and was pronounced out for the season, it seemed everyone in Northern California knew specifically what was wrong with Montana: a torn pronator teres tendon. In the San Francisco Bay Area, the pronator teres joined cable cars, sourdough bread, the Golden Gate bridge, and Alcatraz as prominent regional landmarks – only with more news coverage. Some fans wept when they learned the severity of Montana's injury. Midway through the 1991 season, Rice felt like joining them.

Steve Young had replaced Montana, and the adjustment to another quarterback was difficult for Rice. Young was a left-hander, which meant his passes rotated differently. He loved to scramble, a trait that frustrated not only defenders, but 49ers linemen and receivers, who sometimes had no idea where Young was. He occasionally forced passes into coverage. And he had yet to perfect the art of reading defenses: If Montana's ability to decipher coverages was akin to reading James Joyce, Young was still sifting through *James and the Giant Peach*.

Montana had been hurt before, and Rice had endured his share of backup quarterbacks: Matt Cavanaugh, Jeff Kemp, Mike Moroski, Steve Bono, and Young all had thrown him touchdown passes. But with Montana's future uncertain, this was a major transition for the 49ers and for Rice. In his first season with Young, the growing pains were obvious.

"It was very difficult because with Steve, he's a great talent, but you knew that you had to get open," Rice says. "So that put additional pressure on me to get open real quickly, because if I didn't, Steve likes to create, so he would run the ball. That different rotation on the football was hard, too. It's something that I'm still trying to adjust to."

In keeping with his nature, Rice sought to deal with the adjustment through hard work. He commissioned the 49ers' assistant equipment manager, Ted Walsh, to throw him hundreds of passes each day after practice. Ted Walsh, no relation to Bill, has a decent arm, but more

"I can't think of another player that more exemplifies the drive, work habits and commitment it takes to reach the top."

Mike Holmgren,
Head Coach, Green Bay Packers,
49ers assistant coach from 1986-91

Facing page: *Rice's career had soared at the receiving end of Joe Montana's passes. Starting with the 1991 season, he had to make the adjustment to Steve Young's delivery.*

importantly, he's a lefty. Rice worked Walsh's arm until it was ready to fall off, but the switch to Young remained a struggle. Eventually, Young and Rice would go on to become one of the most prolific passing combinations in NFL history, one which would produce more scoring plays than Montana and Rice. In the beginning, however, they were a mismatch.

The 49ers lost four of their first six games in 1991, and it was in the season's fifth week that the frustration seemed to crystallize. The 49ers visited the L.A. Coliseum for a date with the Raiders. Two longtime San Francisco stars, safety Ronnie Lott and halfback Roger Craig, had signed with the Raiders over the off-season after being left unprotected by the 49ers in Plan B free agency. Young was skittish and imprecise against the physical Raiders defense, and Rice felt some of the side effects. Young threw several high passes that Rice jumped for, leaving him vulnerable to big hits from Raiders defenders, including the unrelenting Lott. On one play Rice soared for an errant pass and had his feet knocked out from under him by cornerback Terry McDaniel. He made a perfectly straight landing … right on his head. It looked awkward and scary, and the crowd gasped. "For a split second, I felt this little stinging sensation going down my arm," Rice recalls. "But I was laughing, because it was sort of exciting."

But no one in the 49ers' locker room was laughing after the game, which ended in a 12-6 defeat. The season was unraveling. The 49ers were 4-5 after Young went down with a knee injury against the Atlanta Falcons, and Bono, in his first NFL start, failed to produce a touchdown drive in a 10-3 defeat at New Orleans the following

week. It was around this time that Rice revealed he had suffered a torn posterior cruciate ligament in his right knee during the second game of the season. The injury would have kept many players sidelined for several weeks or more, but Rice didn't even consider sitting. He had never missed a game due to injury on any level and didn't intend to establish a precedent.

The 49ers were 4-6; the season was a disaster. And then a crazy thing happened: the team caught fire. Their offense began to thrive under Bono, whose style resembled that of the steady, thoughtful Montana. They won five consecutive games before Young returned from his knee injury. They were 9-6, and no one wanted to face them in the playoffs. Fortunately for the rest of the league, San Francisco didn't qualify for postseason play – for the first and only time in Rice's career. With Young back in command, they closed the season with a 52-14 victory over the playoff-bound Chicago Bears at Candlestick Park.

Rice's year ended with 80 receptions, 1,206 yards and 14 touchdowns – great numbers for most players, but not by his standards. It was around this time that Rice began to change his persona from quiet soldier to vocal warrior. With Lott and Craig relocated, and Montana out of commission, there was a sudden leadership void. Rice had always led by example, but now, with three members of the so-called "Big Four" removed from the locker room, he found himself speaking up both to teammates and to the media. "There was a changing of the guard," says Eric Davis. "He went from a quiet guy who never said anything and just did his job to a guy who felt like it was his time, who felt like he could speak out for what he believed in."

Facing page and above: *After sweating out the only non-playoff season of his career in 1991, Rice found himself emerging as the conscience of the team. "I don't think it's something that you evolve into," he says. "It has to be something that just happens naturally."*

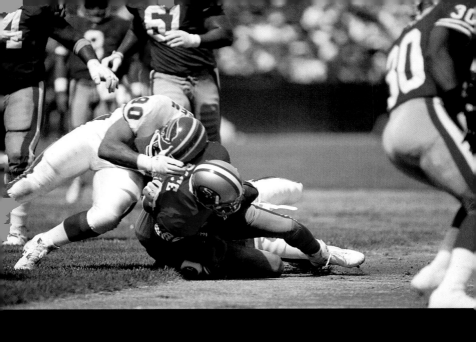

At first, Rice's delivery was coarse and unrefined. Earlier in his career, he had hired a speech coach to improve his diction and grammar. But after a game, Rice's passion often caused him to snap. Several times his postgame comments reflected anger over his lack of involvement in the offense. "We all grow in this game," says Denver Broncos coach Mike Shanahan, the 49ers' offensive coordinator from 1992 to 1994. "Sometimes I think he would say some things – and he was speaking from the heart – but he didn't understand the repercussions."

Some journalists and fans began to regard Rice as selfish and conceited, though his teammates knew better. "There are some things that have been said about Jerry by people who don't necessarily know what he's about," Davis says. "Jerry's not nearly as bad as people think he is. The cockiness – that's every football player. We all think we're invincible, and we all have an ego. But he also cares about his teammates. He wants them to do well for themselves and for their families."

As time wore on, Rice became the conscience of the 49ers, voicing sentiments that existed in the locker room because he was perhaps the one player in a position to take a stand.

"There was a time when his insecurity was a little debilitating for everyone around him, because he was so driven," Young says. "There's really a strength now to what he does. Instead of just the consummate player, he's now the consummate leader. Sometimes he'll sense that he needs to stand up for the guys, so he'll take what's being talked about and say it in a nice way. I'll lean on him a lot of times. I'll say, 'This is what's going on,' and he'll pass it on to the coaches or management.

People really respect him, and when he says something, it's hard to dispute."

Even when Rice was directly critical of the organization – as he was when Montana was traded following the 1992 season – his superiors respected his opinions. "I don't think anything he says is really detrimental to the well-being of the team," Eddie DeBartolo says. "When he talks, people respect his views and opinions, and hold him in high esteem." Says Carmen Policy: "He doesn't discriminate. If it's a player, if it's a situation involving another team, if it's the 49ers, and most of all if it's himself, he'll call it the way he sees it. When you have that kind of consistency and objectivity, coupled with an unparalleled commitment to perfect performance, you take it as a strength rather than a weakness."

Rice's leadership role expanded in 1992. Though Montana's elbow problems flared up again, keeping him out for all but the second half of the final regular-season game, the 49ers were able to thrive. Young settled down, won his second consecutive passing title and put together an MVP season as the 49ers stormed to a league-best 14-2 record. Their only two regular-season defeats had mitigating circumstances: a 24-14 setback at Phoenix in which Young barely played because of the flu, and a 34-31 home loss to Buffalo that Rice scarcely remembers. That's because he was hit so hard after one catch, he was actually snoring on the field. Team doctors woke him up, diagnosed him with a concussion and held him out for the rest of the game.

"There's a huge gap in that game that I don't remember," Rice says. "The doctors told me later they were asking me questions like what cereal I had for

---

Facing page: *The scariest moment of Rice's career: Driven into the turf by Buffalo's Phil Hansen, Rice is knocked cold before being assisted by trainer Lindsy McLean.* **Above:** *He's still woozy when the 49ers' team physician, Dr. Michael Dillingham, walks him off the field.*

breakfast – I don't remember any of that. I was completely gone. The guys told me I was snoring, right there on the ground. When they took me to the sidelines, I was drooling. I sort of woke up in the locker room asking, 'What happened?' and that was real scary."

Rice is proud that of all the hits he has taken, this is the only one that knocked him cold. He normally springs up from jarring collisions, as if to show the defender, "You can't hurt me." In fact, Rice is often the aggressor. He is a fierce blocker who has knocked many an unsuspecting defender on his butt. On some of the 49ers' biggest plays over the past 12 years – including the catch-and-runs of 92 and 95 yards by John Taylor in a stirring Monday Night Football victory over the L.A. Rams in 1989 – Rice has delivered huge blocks to help the cause.

"When you throw a block, that's your only time to get back at the defensive backs," Rice says. "You can let him know that you're not gonna tolerate any intimidation or anything like that. If I see a linebacker 255 pounds chasing a running back and I have a chance to hit him, I'm gonna hit him straight in his chest. It's just getting rid of some frustration. It's something the defensive backs have to think about, and it keeps them off guard. Because when a defensive back is right up in front of you, he doesn't expect you to come up and light into him. He expects you to put a little move on him or run him off. But you line up in front of me, I'm gonna try to take your head off."

Former NFL tight end Jamie Williams, Rice's teammate with the 49ers from 1989 to 1993, remembers a conversation the two had before one home game. "The first 15 plays were always scripted, and the first play was either going to be a run, where I was to the point of attack, or a pass to him. Jerry comes jumping around the locker room and says, 'Hey, man, you know what I hope? I hope they run that running play on the first play.' One of the cornerbacks on the other team had talked some trash in the paper, and Jerry wanted to get him. He said, 'I want to hit that guy in the mouth as hard as I can, just so he knows where I'm coming from. You watch me, I'm gonna come right off the ball and hit him right in the mouth.' So sure enough we run the running play, and Jerry smacks this guy. I can still see Jerry jogging back to the huddle, his helmet all crooked, flashing a little smile."

It would have been tempting to anoint Rice the best blocking receiver around, except there was an even better one in the same huddle: Taylor, who played alongside Rice from 1987 to 1995. The two would engage in friendly competitions to see who could deliver the most punishing hits on defenders. The day after a game, they'd sit in meeting rooms watching films and scanning for big hits, making boasts like, "Look at how I knocked him down. His head hit the ground before his feet did."

Says Taylor, who retired after the 1995 season: "I used to be a defensive back [in high school], and I was used to hitting people, so it came naturally to me. We took blocking very seriously on that team. Just because we were receivers, it wasn't like we wouldn't get in there and mix it up. I figured a defensive player was gonna take any shot at me he could get, so I'd try to take him out early and let him know it's gonna be a long day."

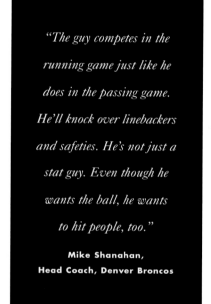

"The guy competes in the running game just like he does in the passing game. He'll knock over linebackers and safeties. He's not just a stat guy. Even though he wants the ball, he wants to hit people, too."

**Mike Shanahan,
Head Coach, Denver Broncos**

Facing page: *Rice often runs away from defenders, but he can also dish out punishment. Part of his greatness is his ability to gain yardage after making the catch.*

"When you're on that football field, you can't be a nice guy. I can't shake hands before a game. Even if I know you, if we talk over the phone, when I take the football field it's not about being friends. It's very hard for me when I see guys go over and talk to each other and stuff like that. After the game, I can shake hands with someone and we can congratulate each other, but before the game, no way." **Jerry Rice**

Left: Rice's off-field personality can be engaging, but he's not very approachable before, during, or immediately after a game.
Above: Even when he's sitting on the sidelines, Rice always keeps his head in the game.

Though they were never close off the field, Rice and Taylor formed one of the most dangerous receiving tandems in NFL history, right up there with the Pittsburgh Steelers' dynamic duo of the seventies, Lynn Swann and John Stallworth. JR and JT, as they became known to teammates, were a sort of odd couple, at least in terms of work habits. To Rice, practice is religion. To Taylor, it was a drag. "He worked hard," Taylor says of Rice, "and I was the opposite." What they shared was a knack for summoning heroic degrees of fortitude on Sundays.

"People don't realize it, but he's probably just as talented as I am," Rice says. "He didn't get all the recognition, and he never said anything. He just did his job, made great plays, and took a lot of pressure off of me, and I give him all the credit. Because without JT, there's no way I would have broken all the records. He's a character. I have never seen a time when JT was really serious. It probably would be scary. He never showed that he was nervous. He would go into a ball game all relaxed, like it was just another day. He never stretched before games; he'd just go out there and start running. He never conditioned during the off-season. I'd work my butt off, and this guy would sit around during the off-season, just enjoying life. Then he'd go into the season and take care of business."

Another receiver who earned Rice's deepest admiration was Steve Largent, who starred for the Seahawks from 1976 to 1989 and later earned induction into the Hall of Fame. Like Rice, Largent was not considered fast, but inevitably managed to break free for long gains. Now a U.S. Congressman from Oklahoma, Largent retired after 14 seasons with an NFL-record 100 receiving touchdowns, one better than Green Bay Packers Hall of Famer Don Hutson.

"When I was a kid, I was inspired by guys like Drew Pearson and Tony Hill of the Cowboys, and John Stallworth and Lynn Swann," Rice says. "I love the way Swann would fly through the air and make those incredible catches. He wasn't a real fast guy but ran great routes, just like Steve Largent, who ran great routes and had great hands. Whenever we played Seattle I would make it my purpose to watch him from the sidelines when they had the ball. I would watch him run routes because he had a true talent."

That's why it blew Rice away that in his eighth NFL season, he was on the verge of breaking Largent's record. He caught touchdown no. 100 at Candlestick on November 29, 1992 against the Philadelphia Eagles. The next week, the 49ers hosted the Miami Dolphins, and Rice dragged the suspense out until the fourth quarter. Then, on third-and-goal from the 12, he flashed across the end zone, got a step on cornerback J. B. Brown and caught a lively pass from Young to claim the record.

For years, Rice had been touted by experts as "possibly the greatest receiver of all time." Now he was starting to lose the "possibly." But Rice wasn't consumed with his place in history as much as he was his team's. With four Super Bowl titles, the 49ers had been the undisputed Team of the Eighties. Now they were hoping to become the first NFL dynasty of the modern era to sustain its dominance into a second decade. The Niners had missed a chance to become the first team to win three consecutive Super Bowls, losing the 1990 NFC Championship game at Candlestick Park to the New

Above: Though their approaches were opposite, Rice and Taylor shared a penchant for big plays and displays of mettle.
Facing page: (clockwise from top left) Rice catches his 100th career touchdown against the Eagles in 1992; breaks free in the 1993 season opener at Pittsburgh; gives coaches the scoop during a four-touchdown day at Tampa Bay later that year; and confers with Steve Young in a December 1993 game at Detroit.

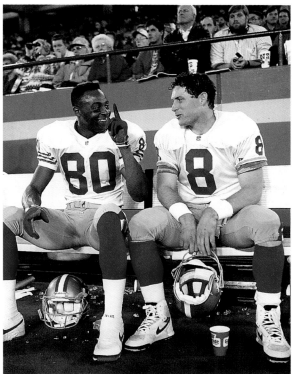

"What a lot of guys don't understand about Jerry is that with him, football's a 12-month thing. When other people slow down in the eighth or ninth game, he picks it up. He separates himself from the others because of his stamina. He's a natural, but he still works. That's what separates the good from the great."

Kevin Smith, Cornerback, Dallas Cowboys

York Giants, 15-13, on a last-second field goal. Now, two years later, the team standing in San Francisco's way was Dallas. The Cowboys had been put together masterfully by head coach Jimmy Johnson and were considered the league's up-and-coming power as the 1992 playoffs began. The 49ers and Cowboys each won divisional playoff games to set up the first matchup of what would become the most gripping rivalry in professional sports, the equivalent of the Lakers-Celtics clashes of the eighties.

It was the 49ers and the Cowboys for the NFC Championship at Candlestick on January 17, 1993, and the home team wanted to make a strong opening statement. On the game's third play from scrimmage, Young dropped back and floated a deep pass over the middle to Rice, who had burned Dallas cornerback Issiac Holt. Rice caught it in stride and raced 63 yards for a touchdown. The crowd went nuts, but not in the way Rice had hoped. While Rice was high-fiving fans in the back of the end zone, the rest of the crowd was reacting to a yellow penalty flag – for a holding call on 49ers guard Guy McIntyre.

That set the tone, alright. The 49ers turned the ball over four times, and the Cowboys rolled to a 30-20 victory. Rice caught eight passes for 123 yards, including a five-yard touchdown in the fourth quarter that was his NFL-playoff-record 13th scoring reception, but it wasn't enough.

The next season Rice acted as if he were in a constant bad mood, which was not good news for defensive backs. Reporters who covered the 49ers had learned long before to get their quotes from Rice early in the week, because the closer it got to game day, the grumpier Rice became. "Even my wife knows that by Thursday or Friday, I'm gonna get in that mood, so she doesn't even come near me," Rice says. In 1993, Rice reacted to what he perceived as negative media coverage by instituting a temporary boycott, refusing to speak with reporters for two weeks. His game, as usual, spoke volumes.

Rice caught 98 passes for 1,503 yards and 15 touchdowns during the regular season and was named the NFL's Offensive Player of the Year. On one sizzling November Sunday in Tampa, Rice burned the Buccaneers for four touchdowns. He was also voted by teammates as the winner of the Len Eshmont Award, given annually to the team's most inspirational and courageous player. Rice had won the award in 1987, but he was shocked to win it a second time. When head coach George Seifert called out his name at the end of practice to tell him he'd won, Rice thought he was about to be cursed out for goofing off in the background.

"It meant a lot," Rice says, "because it's voted on by your teammates, and it's all about respect. So it's good to know that your teammates support you and respect you and appreciate the things that you do. It's something you'll never forget. When this is all over, people aren't gonna look back and think about all the games they won and stuff like that. They'll think about the people they went to battle with and the respect they had for each other."

The 49ers went 10-6 and then destroyed the New York Giants in their first playoff game by a 44-3 score, setting up an NFC Championship rematch with the Cowboys, this time at Texas Stadium. There were some pregame barbs traded back and forth between Rice and Kevin Smith, the Cowboys' talented young cornerback

Facing page and above: *Rice and the 49ers met a wall of resistance in the 1992 NFC Championship game against the Cowboys, who emerged as the 49ers' chief rival of the nineties.*

82

"There are others that have the same dogged determination and perseverance but aren't able to do things because physically, they can't. But I don't even think there's been a guy equal to him physically – even a so-called non-achiever, somebody where people would say, 'God, he'd have been great, if only he'd had a better attitude ...' There isn't even one of those."

Bill Walsh, Hall of Fame Coach

who had held him without a touchdown during the teams' regular-season meeting, a 26-17 Dallas victory. Rice was already steaming, and then Johnson, the Cowboys' coach, ignited an emotional inferno, proclaiming on a live radio appearance, "We will win the ball game, and you can put it in three-inch headlines."

The 49ers were livid when they took the field, and the Cowboys added fuel to their fire. As the 49ers gathered in the end zone for pregame introductions, Dallas players broke into their huddle and began taunting them. There was pushing, shoving, and woofing on both sides. Smith got in Rice's face and said, "Just gonna be me and you all day." Rice never talks to opponents before the game – he didn't even say hi to Montana when the 49ers played Kansas City early in the 1994 season – and he wanted no part of Smith. When Smith extended his arm for a handshake, Rice made a gesture that, loosely translated, indicated Smith should get lost. During the coin-flip ceremony, Cowboys defensive end Charles Haley, Rice's former teammate, told him not to pay attention to the exuberance of the younger Cowboys. Haley offered his hand and Rice wouldn't shake that, either. Then Dallas's honorary captain, Hall of Fame quarterback Roger Staubach, reached out to shake Rice's hand. Staubach had been one of Rice's favorite players growing up, but Rice just stared at him. Finally, begrudgingly, Rice shook Staubach's hand.

"I look at what the Cowboys did as showing no respect, none at all," Rice says. "Their attitude was, 'We don't care, you guys are beaten already.' With Johnson making that prediction, it really caught me and the organization by surprise. As for the handshaking stuff, my

thought was, 'Come on, this is professional football here. We don't have to do all that.'"

The Cowboys backed up their brashness with a 38-21 victory en route to their second consecutive Super Bowl crown. Smith frustrated Rice again, holding him to six catches for 83 yards and no touchdowns. At one point Rice grew so frustrated with Smith's trash-talking that he shoved the cornerback after a play and was flagged for a personal foul. Rice felt Smith wasn't giving him respect, but in fact the opposite was true.

"Some guys you can play straight-up, but if you try that with Jerry, you're dead," Smith explains. "With Jerry, you have to find another way to beat him. What I've always tried with him is to get his mind off the game. I like to talk and push and aggravate, but it's nothing personal. The guy's so tough to play against. He's so great off the line that if you want to press him, he'll push you off of him. You try to mirror him, and he shakes you. You try to be aggressive, and he'll slap you down. You try playing off of him, and he freezes you with a move. I don't know if there's one solution physically, so you have to go after him mentally."

Mentally, Rice was devastated by the defeat. Disenchanted with the lack of commitment from some of the 49ers' younger players, frustrated by the organization's inability to silence the Cowboys, he briefly considered retirement. But Rice, as he always seems to, chose to fight rather than quit.

As the 1994 season approached, Rice made two loud non-verbal statements. First he showed up at the 49ers' training camp in Rocklin, California two days before veterans were required to report, joining an awed collection of rookies and free agents for two-a-day practices in 100-

---

Above: *The Dallas cornerbacks stayed in Rice's face all game long.* **Facing page:** *Rice told his teammates that beating Dallas was a point of pride and tried to set an early tone in the 1993 NFC Championship game. But the 49ers came up empty two years in a row.*

"Has he become more of a leader? Yes, absolutely. He has matured immensely over the period of time that I've known him. He'll talk to the team before a big game, or any game. Or if we lose and he feels the team didn't put out the way it should, he's probably the first to reprimand the team. And people really listen to him — they'll hear him before they hear the coach sometimes — because here's a guy, one of their own, that does it balls out all the time. When he gets on them, it means something.

He has total credibility."

George Seifert, Head Coach, 49ers

degree heat. It was a sign of Rice's commitment to overtaking the Cowboys, and he was not alone. Young had studied up on the offense like never before. Policy's ingenuity and DeBartolo's wallet had allowed the 49ers to finesse the NFL's salary cap and sign more than a half-dozen free agents, including defensive ends Richard Dent and Rickey Jackson, and linebackers Ken Norton and Gary Plummer.

The 49ers were so strapped for salary-cap room they could not afford a five-man practice squad. Then Rice, who two years earlier had endured a protracted contract fight during training camp, made his second statement. He gave back $170,000 worth of incentive clauses – performance incentives he would easily attain by season's end – in order to fund the practice squad. "I was just giving something back," Rice says. "I've been very fortunate, had so many great years and made plenty of money. And I felt like we needed those guys to get us ready. It was weird because the practice-squad guys all came up to thank me. I hadn't even thought of it that way."

The 49ers weren't done spending. Two weeks later, they plucked the biggest free-agent prize of all: All-Pro cornerback Deion Sanders, who during his years with the Atlanta Falcons had provided Rice with his toughest battles. Rice had openly worried whether Sanders's flamboyance would fly amid the buttoned-down atmosphere of the 49ers, and team executives gave him a chance to veto the deal. Rice cast his vote for Sanders, and "Prime Time's" appearance helped transform the 49ers' personality into a more extroverted, flashy mode.

Before Sanders arrived, Rice got the season off with a

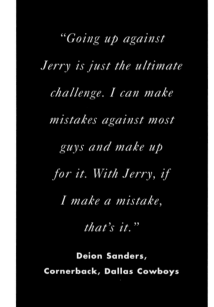

"Going up against Jerry is just the ultimate challenge. I can make mistakes against most guys and make up for it. With Jerry, if I make a mistake, that's it."

Deion Sanders, Cornerback, Dallas Cowboys

bang. The 49ers were hosting the L.A. Raiders, the team that had stifled them three years earlier, and the only team against which Rice had never scored. The Raiders still enjoyed a huge following in the Bay Area dating back to their Oakland days; as it turned out, they would move back to Oakland before the next season. However, their trip north to begin the 1994 campaign on Monday Night Football was a fiasco. The 49ers won 44-14, but that's not what people will remember years from now. Instead, they'll recall the game as the one in which Jerry Rice set his most amazing record.

Going into the game, Rice had scored 124 career touchdowns, two short of the all-time mark held by former Cleveland Browns great, Jim Brown. The amazing thing was that Brown played running back, meaning he had far more opportunities to touch the ball than a receiver like Rice. Some people call Brown the greatest football player of all time. Rice put in his bid for such consideration when he broke Brown's record.

Rice derived extra motivation from the pregame hype surrounding the Raiders' legion of speedy receivers. "You want speed?" he seemed to say. On the 49ers' fourth play of the game, he took a Young pass over the middle, broke a tackle and busted loose for a 69-yard touchdown pass. With 12:15 left in the fourth quarter, Rice ran 23 yards on a reverse to tie Brown with touchdown no. 126. The game was a blowout, and Rice figured he was through for the night. But then word came down from Shanahan, who was sitting in the upstairs coaches' box: "Jerry, we're gonna give you one shot."

The 49ers had the ball at the Raiders' 38 with just over four minutes remaining.

Facing page: *The Raiders were the only team Rice had never scored against until the 1994 season opener, when he scored three touchdowns to break Jim Brown's record.*

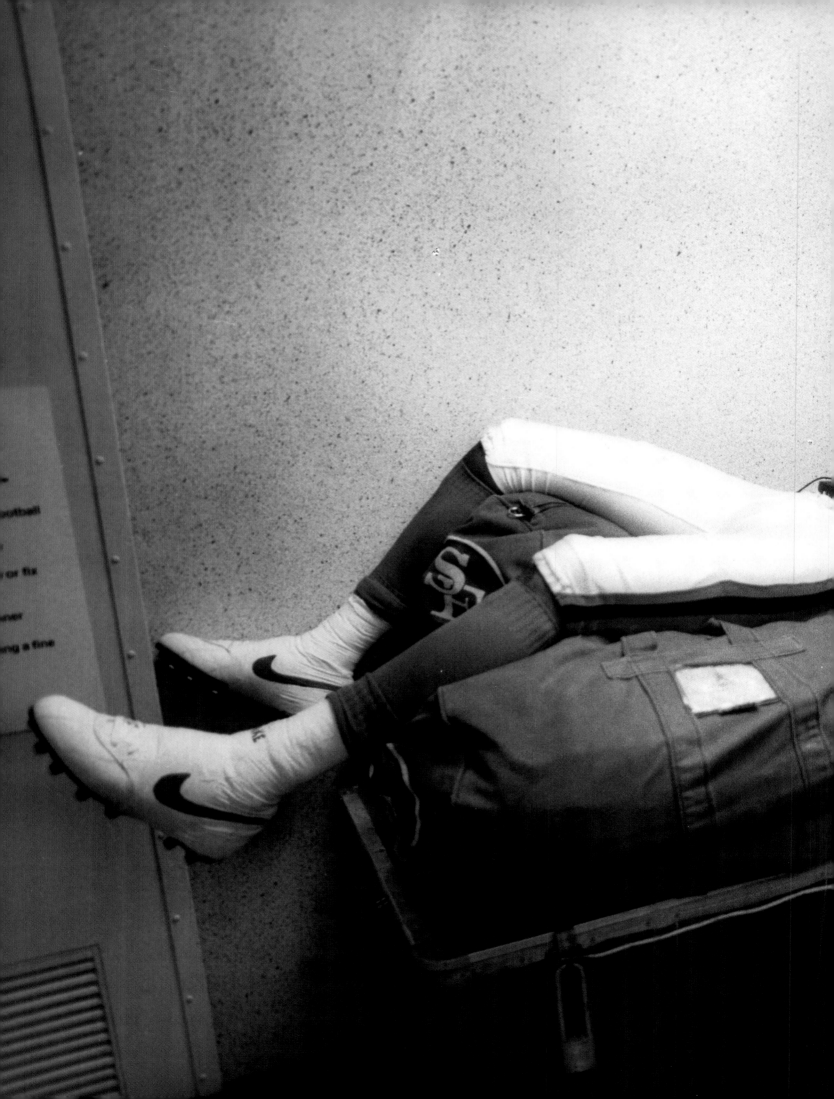

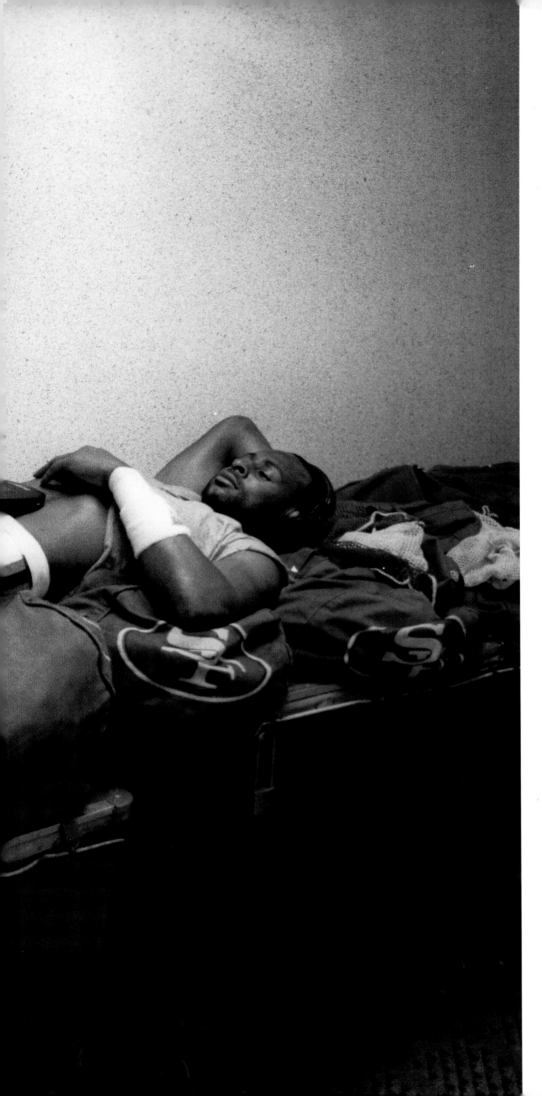

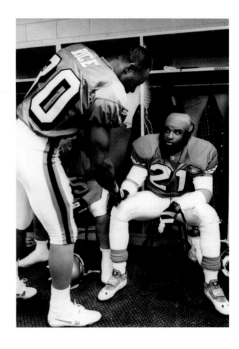

"Before, Deion would just rely on his speed, but the amazing thing about him now is he's more physical. He makes you work hard off the line of scrimmage and then he'll run with you. The worst part is when you've got him beat, and you know you've got him beat, but the ball is not right there out in front of you. That's the worst feeling, because you know he'll catch up. A lot of people say he doesn't have the stats or that his game has shortcomings, but they're wrong; he's probably the best ever to play the game." **Jerry Rice**

Left: Pregame, Rice's focus is absolute. He visualizes success in the game ahead. So far, that vision has been 20/20.
Above: When they were teammates in San Francisco in 1994, Rice's style clashed with the flashier Deion Sanders. But both agreed on a common cause: winning.

"The ball's going up," Young told Rice in the huddle, "so just find it and take it in." Rice nodded, went in motion and ran a post toward the goal line, where he and a crowd of defensive backs saw a ball that seemed to hang in the air forever. "The way it happened was unreal," Rice says. "The ball was floating up in the air and it was like everything just stopped for a split-second. The rest was in slow motion." Rice's mind flashed back to what one of his early receivers coaches with the 49ers, current Minnesota Vikings head coach Dennis Green, had taught him: Always attack the ball at its highest point; don't wait for it to come to you. So Rice went up and grabbed it at the two yard line and lunged past cornerback Albert Lewis into the end zone, where it seemed like the entire Raiders' secondary fell on top of him, everyone slapping and tugging at the ball long after the touchdown had been signaled. "It was the ideal scenario," Rice says. "Somehow, that's the record that really stands out the most. I didn't really expect to break it that night."

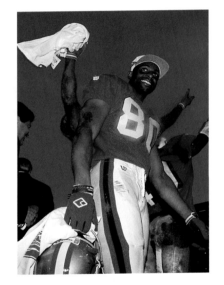

Afterwards, Jim Brown told the *San Francisco Chronicle*, "I feel it's a great thing for modern football for Jerry Rice to get such a record. It's a real record, a top-flight record, a record that has value. It was established in the context of Super Bowl teams and potential Super Bowl teams. This is a legitimate, *legitimate* record."

As if there were any doubt, Rice went out and caught a career-high 112 passes for 1,499 yards and 13 touchdowns during the regular season, including a 57-yard scoring play in the 49ers' landmark, 21-14 victory over the Cowboys in November. That game helped the 49ers go 13-3 and gain homefield advantage throughout the playoffs. Their third straight meeting with Dallas to decide the NFC Championship was played at Candlestick, and Rice knew things would be different before the game even began.

When Rice came out for pregame warm-ups, he noticed several Cowboys players stretching on the north end of the field. "That's our end of the field," Rice thought to himself. "Alright, here we go again." Rice ran right at Cowboys safety James Washington, gave a quick fake, stopped just short of him and stared him down. Then Rice went back behind the 49ers' bench to work the fans into a frenzy. When some of the younger, more emotional 49ers came out of the locker room – particularly running backs Ricky Watters and William Floyd – they broke into a straight-out sprint and began pushing the Cowboys off their turf. "You know what?" Rice says. "I knew the game was won. That set the tone right there."

Sure enough, the 49ers jumped on the Cowboys, forcing three quick turnovers and rolling to a 21-0 lead. But the proud Dallas team, led by quarterback Troy Aikman and receiver Michael Irvin, fought back to 24-14 with 1:56 left in the first half. The teams traded punts, and San Francisco took over with less than a minute to go. Some teams might have elected to run out the clock, but the 49ers went for the kill. They got to the Dallas 28, where Young dropped back and placed one of the prettiest passes you'll ever see – Montana-style – over Rice's head and into his outstretched hands. Rice, who had beaten cornerback Larry Brown to the left rear corner of the end zone, pulled it down with eight seconds remaining, and the 49ers, who went on to win 38-28, were firmly in command. "That was a play we needed because, before that, you could

Above: *Rice's touchdown just before halftime gave the 49ers a lift in their '94 NFC Championship game victory over the Cowboys.*
Facing page: *In their lucky "throwback" jerseys, the 49ers and Rice finally beat the Cowboys in the 1994 regular season.*
Following pages: *Rice, Young and a few thousand friends share in the celebration.*

"When I look at him and I analyze what he does and I see how he approaches his game – and his life,
because I think the game is his life – I develop these feelings of inadequacy. It's almost as though he
operates on a different level. He goes out at night with Zeus, while the rest of us
wallow down in the valley with mere mortals."

Carmen Policy, President, 49ers

feel the momentum starting to change," Rice says. "They probably thought we would try to set up a field goal, but we went for the nail in the coffin. I think that one play right there broke them, big-time. I don't think anybody could have thrown that ball any better than that. On that play I didn't hear or see anything but the ball. I didn't hear the crowd or the defensive back until I came down with the ball, and then it was like someone turned on the noise."

Two weeks later Rice suited up for Super Bowl XXIX at Joe Robbie Stadium, site of his MVP performance in Super Bowl XXIII. The 49ers were heavy favorites to defeat San Diego, and Young and Rice robbed the game of most of its suspense in the first 84 seconds. On the 49ers' third play from scrimmage, Young faked a handoff to William Floyd and threw deep over the middle to Rice, who had split the Chargers' safeties, Stanley Richard and Darren Carrington. He caught the ball and raced into the end zone untouched for a 44-yard touchdown, completing the quickest opening-touchdown drive in Super Bowl history. It got worse for San Diego, which went on to lose by a 49-26 score.

"The thing was, he and I probably hadn't had a ball hit the ground in practice for a month, maybe longer," Young says. "We got into this incredible groove, and when the game came we felt like we could do anything we wanted."

On the 49ers' third possession, Rice suffered a badly strained shoulder while being tackled by Chargers cornerback Darrien Gordon on an end around, and went to the locker room to be evaluated. He was in severe pain, and it would take him months to completely recover. But nothing short of amputation could keep Rice out of this game. He returned to catch two more touchdowns – the last one, a seven-yarder early in the fourth quarter, gave Young, the game's MVP, his sixth touchdown pass of the day, breaking Montana's Super Bowl record. Rice finished with 10 receptions for 149 yards and a big hug from Young, who finally had extricated himself from the shadow of Montana's legend. "Jerry Rice with one arm is better than everyone in the league with two arms," Young said after the game.

The next day, Rice got on a plane for Hawaii, where he was scheduled to start in the Pro Bowl for the ninth consecutive year. The shoulder kept him from playing, but just the fact that Rice was there was amazing. Many marquee players skip the Pro Bowl with minor or phantom injuries, but in Rice's eyes, "If there's a game scheduled, I'm gonna show up. The people you compete against vote you into the Pro Bowl, and it's a matter of pride for me to compete."

Rice's peers appreciate his presence in Hawaii. Says Packers coach Mike Holmgren, who presided over the NFC squad following the 1995 season: "At the Pro Bowl, when he runs his routes in practice, everyone stops and watches. That's just the way it is."

In the wake of his third Super Bowl triumph, Rice showed signs of slowing down. Not on the football field, where he remained as active and nimble as ever in his mid-30s. Not in his training regimen, which if anything became more intense. But in his mind and in his soul, Rice began traveling at a comfortable pace, one which afforded him the opportunity to achieve the internal satisfaction that had always eluded him.

Facing page: *Rice was smiling from the start of Super Bowl XXIX, scoring three touchdowns from MVP Young despite a painful shoulder injury.*
Above: *For the first time in five years, Rice held the Vince Lombardi Trophy in triumph.*

"For a long time it was fear of failure that drove me," Rice says. "Now I think it's just the love for the game. You reach a point where it's not about the money or the endorsements, it's just the enjoyment of the sport itself."

Says Young: "He is so driven to be the best, and what I love about him is, once it became clear he *was* the best, he changed. Instead of putting on a false 'I'm not the best' persona, he accepted it and redirected the challenge. He carries himself like he's the best ever; he's not afraid to do that. He's very comfortable with just being Jerry Rice. And now I think his mission is, 'Forget everyone else, I'm gonna see how far I can take being the best. Because no one's ever gone this far before.' "

This is not to say that Rice has snuffed out the fire within. He still gets emotional, and he still speaks from the heart. Following the 49ers' second game of the 1995 season, a 41-10 victory over the Atlanta Falcons at Candlestick Park, Rice erupted in the locker room. In a profanity-laced tirade that made all the sports highlight shows, Rice scolded reporters for what he believed was their overemphasis of Sanders's role in the 49ers' championship season the year before. Sanders had signed with the Cowboys, and though Rice meant not to offend him but to demand credit for the 49ers' other defensive players, it added tension to their relationship. Things had been strained since the Wednesday before Super Bowl XXIX, when Rice and Sanders had quarreled over the severity of a curfew violation by a large group of 49ers – Rice arguing for a more serious mind-set, Sanders for more of a hang-loose approach.

Rice had been prepared to restructure his contract to enable the 49ers to re-sign Sanders in 1995. When Sanders signed with the Cowboys for $35 million over seven years and then said he left San Francisco because he wasn't appreciated, Rice took exception.

"I never had anything against Deion," Rice says. "He did his own thing. But I think the thing about Deion is, he has to be The Man. He has to be the focus. He has to have people around him that really appreciate him. I've respected him for his talent and all that – to me, he's the ultimate challenge, the best cornerback I've ever played against. But some of the things he said when he left here really surprised me. He said we never showed him respect and that we really didn't appreciate him. I thought things were really great. Maybe he wanted us to go out of our way or something, I don't know. Maybe he wanted us to bow to him. I'm sorry, I don't bow to anybody."

Offended by the tone of Rice's outburst following the Falcons game, Sanders lashed back in the days leading up to the 49ers' November 12 game at Dallas. Sanders called Rice "comical" and began imitating his locker-room tirade, complete with exaggerated Mississippi drawl.

Facing page: From his rookie year forward, Rice's 49er teammates looked to him with respect for his on-the-field heroics.

That rubbed Jerry's wife, Jackie, the wrong way. "I remember when Deion also wasn't so polished," she says. "When they first drafted him and he was sitting in a news conference with 1,000 gold chains on, he wasn't as articulate as he is today. I thought it was ignorant on Deion's part to make fun of something like that. Everyone's not like him. Everyone didn't grow up in the 'hood."

After Rice led the 49ers to a stunning, 38-20 victory over the Cowboys with Elvis Grbac subbing for the injured Young, he and Sanders cleared the air and embraced. At that point it looked like the 49ers might defend their Super Bowl title, but it was Dallas which ultimately won out. That the 49ers nearly ended up with home-field advantage throughout the playoffs was a testament to the brilliance of Rice, who steadied the team through Young's absence and cranked up his play even more when the quarterback returned. The Niners' running game had been decimated by the off-season departure of Watters, who signed with the Philadelphia Eagles, and the severe knee injury suffered by William Floyd midway through the season. John Taylor and tight end Brent Jones were also banged up; it was up to Rice to pick up the slack.

In the stirring victory over the Cowboys, Rice left no doubt as to who was the team's driving force. The 49ers, thanks partly to Young's shoulder injury and partly to a two-game losing streak – including a shocking setback at the hands of the expansion Carolina Panthers – came into Texas Stadium as 10-point underdogs. Beating the Cowboys, whose 8-1 record was the NFL's best, looked to be an impossible task. San Francisco hadn't lost three straight in the same year since 1980, and its amazing streak seemed destined to end with the untested Elvis Grbac at quarterback. Things were so bleak that Policy

told his boss, 49ers owner Eddie DeBartolo, not to bother making the trip.

Frustration was inevitable, an explosion likely. It happened at halftime, just as the 49ers were about to go back out onto the field, in a corner of the cramped, damp visitor's locker room: Rice looked into some of his teammates' eyes, noticed the lack of commitment on their faces and pitched a fit.

"Hey, this is —— serious," Rice screamed. "Cut out all this B.S. We haven't won —— yet."

When Rice's scolding was complete, it was so quiet you could hear a jaw drop. After all, the 49ers led 31-7.

They had jumped on Dallas like a pack of bloodhounds and Rice, as usual, was the lead dog. On the game's second play from scrimmage, Rice caught a short pass from Grbac and dashed up the middle of the field for an 81-yard touchdown. By halftime, he had 155 receiving yards – and he had no intention of letting up "People were a little too relaxed," Rice recalls. "They felt like the game was over. You could tell, just from the way they came in and the way they started moving around. They just had that look about them like they were getting ready to stray a little bit. And you never want to get in that predicament right there. I just wanted them to know that we had another half to play and that it could change, that they could get momentum. So we just had to go for the jugular, put this team away while we had the chance."

Recalls Davis: "He wanted that game. He wasn't necessarily screaming at guys because they didn't want the game or weren't intense, it was more of a let's-make-sure tirade. There were things in his head, and maybe they were in everyone's head, and maybe someone needed to say those things."

Facing page: With the 49ers' running game struggling in 1995, people like Atlanta Falcons cornerback D. J. Johnson were all over Rice.
Following pages: Rice's speed isn't blazing by stopwatch standards, but once he gets the ball he is little more than a blur.

runs is full speed."

Rice finished the 1995 season with 122 receptions, which would have been an NFL record had Detroit's Herman Moore not hauled in 123 in the same campaign. Rice's 1,848 receiving yards were an NFL record. He caught 15 touchdown passes, scored once on a run and once on his first career end-zone fumble recovery, increasing his all-time touchdown record to 156. He also threw a touchdown pass – a perfect, 41-yard spiral to rookie J. J. Stokes while being pounded by two Atlanta defenders in the season's final game. He extended his streak of games with at least one catch to 160. By year's end, Rice had become the NFL's career leader in receptions (942, surpassing Art Monk) and receiving yards (15,123, surpassing James Lofton). Many people thought Rice was an ideal choice for league MVP, but that honor went to Packers quarterback Brett Favre, who had thrown an NFC-record 38 touchdown passes. Losing out to Favre was one thing, but losing by a margin of 69 votes to 10 was tough for Rice to swallow.

"I was really surprised, because I felt like I probably had one of my best years, and I didn't come close," Rice says. "Not knocking Brett Favre or anything – he had an exceptional year also, and he deserved to win it. But I think people expect me to just go out and do it every year. They don't realize how much time and hard work that I put into it."

In the 49ers' second-to-last regular-season game, a 37-30 home victory over the Minnesota Vikings on Monday Night Football, Rice caught 14 passes for a career-best 289 yards and three touchdowns. But the 49ers slipped in the season's final week, losing at Atlanta, and drew the Packers as their first playoff opponent at Candlestick Park. As Rice's former offensive coordinator, Green Bay head coach Holmgren knew what had to be done. He based his entire defensive game plan on stopping Rice, sending various defenders to pound him off the line of scrimmage at the expense of other assignments. In essence, he was daring the 49ers to beat the Packers with anyone but Rice, and San Francisco couldn't do it. Double-covered on every play, Rice caught 11 passes for 117 yards, but he gained only 10 yards after the catch. The Packers scored a 27-17 victory, and Rice took it like a man. He made a point of approaching Holmgren in the Packers' locker room and giving him a hug. "It was a very touching moment for me," Holmgren says, "that he would take the time to do that at a time when he must have been so low."

The Green Bay Packers lost the NFC Championship game to the Cowboys, who went on to defeat the Steelers in Super Bowl XXX. The next spring, when the Packers convened for their first mini-camp of the off-season, Holmgren gathered his squad for a speech. He wanted to give them an example of what he wants in a player, of a person who shows the commitment it takes to become a champion. The person he cited was Jerry Rice. "I can't think of another player that more exemplifies the drive, work habits and commitment it takes to reach the top," Holmgren says. "I used Jerry Rice in that speech, and I will continue to do so for my whole career."

Above: *The man who made Breathe Right nasal strips famous has a nose for the end zone, as his still-growing NFL record for career touchdowns attests.* **Facing page:** *When history renders judgment on NFL receivers, one man will stand atop all others: Jerry Rice.*

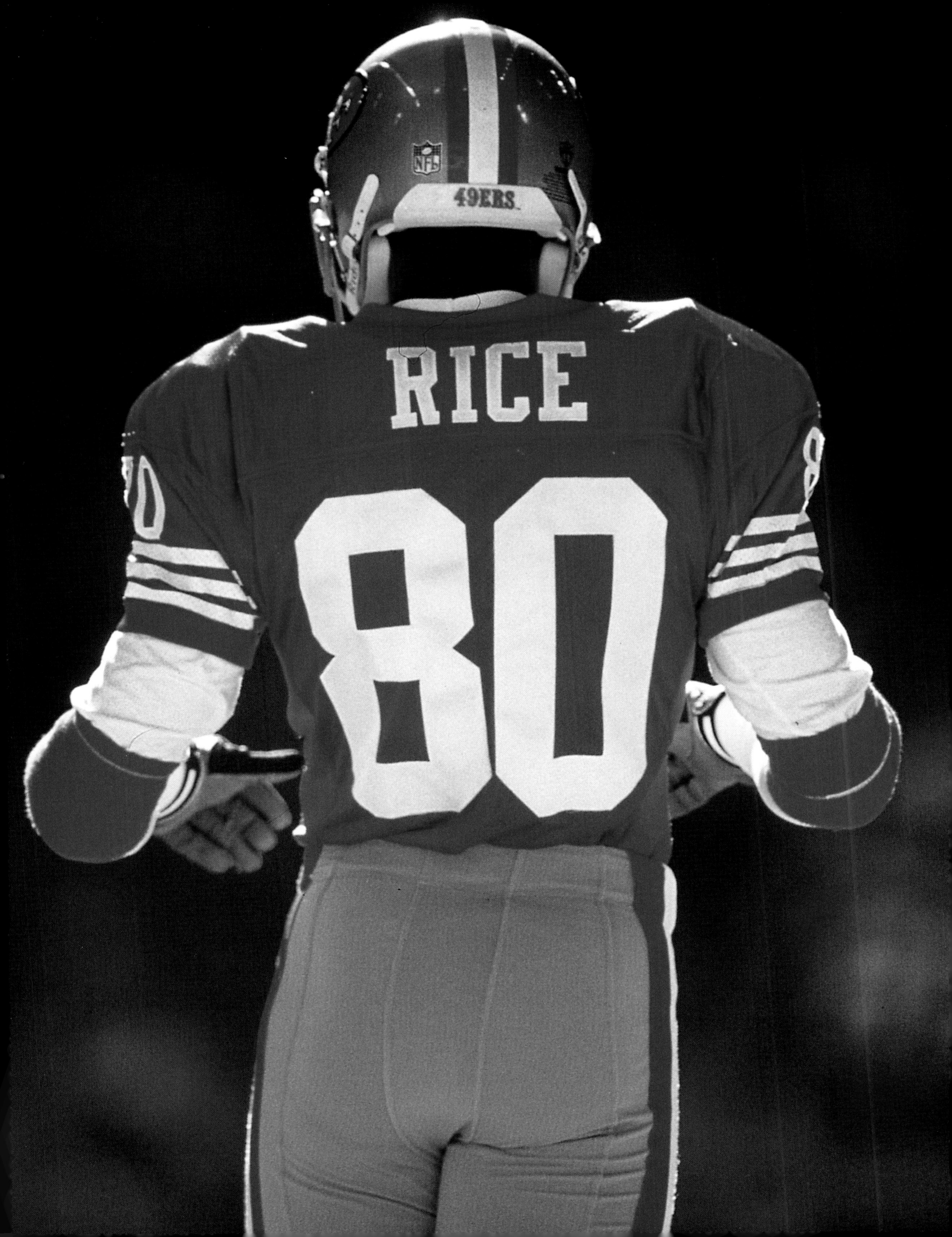
49ERS
RICE
80

King of the Hill

As hills go, it was nothing special: 40 yards from ground to apex, covered with soft Mississippi dirt, pointing upward at a relatively steep grade. Each day after football practice, B. L. Moor High School coach Charles Davis would watch his players – uniforms, pads, and all – sprint up and down the hill 20 times. On one particularly muggy afternoon, Jerry Rice decided 11 sprints were plenty. His heart sank to his stomach, his lungs gasped for air, his legs felt like stacks of wet newspapers. "To hell with this," he said, and began walking toward the locker room.

Rice was going to get away with it, but on his way off the field a voice in his head told him, "Don't quit. Because once you get into that mode of quitting, then you feel like it's OK."

So Rice went back and conquered the hill, and a precedent had been established: The pressure to succeed would come from within, rather than being dictated by others. It's a simple dictum that Rice carried with him all the way to the top – of that little hill back in Crawford, Mississippi, of the 2.5-mile mountain trail that serves as the cornerstone of his off-season training regimen and, not coincidentally, of his profession.

At the highest level of athletic competition, there is a difference between wanting to win and truly needing to win. It's the latter sensation that compels football players to put their bodies in wholly unnatural positions – allowing their limbs to be bent back at 120 degree angles or throwing their bodies into a charging opponent. With Rice, the drive to succeed is so ingrained and so visceral that it transcends even the most determined strivings of his competitors.

When it comes to football, Jerry Rice is committed. In 18 seasons of high school, college, and NFL competition, he has never missed a game. That's remarkable for any player, but for a receiver who routinely absorbs hits from players itching to put him out of commission, it's

phenomenal. "I take as much pride in the fact that I've never missed a game as I do in any of my records."

Rice's teammates know they can never work hard enough, because the best player on the 49ers is always out there working harder.

"When you were a kid, and you were playing junior football or some other sport, there was always one kid on your team who tried harder than the others," says 49ers quarterback Steve Young. "He might not have been the most talented kid, but he would huff and puff, and run extra laps, and do anything he could to help the team win. And the coach would always say, 'If I had a hundred kids like that kid, we'd be world champions.' Well, Jerry Rice is that kid, only taken to an insane degree. It's just that he has so much raw talent, people don't think of him that way. But he's one of those rare people who is the same whether someone's watching or no one's watching. You can come and watch if you want, but he doesn't care, because he's out there working to satisfy something within himself – something none of us can really see."

Nearly two decades after he almost caved in to that glorified mound back in Crawford, Rice is the King of the Hill. That's the title created by his former 49ers teammate Roger Craig, whose insatiable training appetite took him to a county park in San Carlos, California, where a lightly foliated mountain loomed as his tormentor. Under the guidance of training guru Ray Farris, a former Utah State cornerback, Craig began using daily mountain runs to enhance his already masochistic off-season workout program. The mountain serves as a sort of testament to the last 20 years of NFL excellence: Craig inherited his hill-training focus from Hall of Fame running back Walter Payton, who starred for

Above and facing page: *Rice spends his off-seasons trying to keep up with training guru Ray Farris, whose company, All Season Training, is favored by many premier athletes.* **Following pages:** *Rice returns to Mississippi in the summers to work out in the oppressive heat and humidity, which he believes builds character.*

the Chicago Bears from 1975 to 1987; Craig extended his workout group to include another all-time NFL rushing great, Detroit Lions halfback Barry Sanders; Rice came aboard and ultimately succeeded Craig, who retired after the 1993 season, as the group's pacesetter.

Among those who have joined Rice and Farris for their legendary training sessions, either on the mountain or at a local track, include NFL standouts Ricky Watters, Dana Stubblefield, Sean Dawkins, Glyn Milburn, Steve Bono, Mike Sherrard, Jamie Williams, Tom Rathman, Sam Adams, and Darrien Gordon. All-Star guard Mitch Richmond of the NBA's Sacramento Kings and three-time National League Most Valuable Player Barry Bonds of the San Francisco Giants have also spent time with the group.

Farris's basic program, which begins a few days after the end of the 49ers' season, goes like this: For the first eight weeks, the group runs the hill trail every other morning; the other mornings are devoted to work on the track. The run up the hill is especially brisk – Farris is the only person who has done it in less than 15 minutes, with Rice a close second – followed by a steady descent.

The hill work ends after the eighth week. From then on the athletes run daily on the track, where they stretch, run warm-up sprints, and then complete a series of timed sprints at various distances. That is followed by a workout on the football field featuring catching drills and other football exercises and a series of "accelerators" – 100-yard sprints designed to enhance smooth running form. On most days, Rice hits a nearby gym and lifts weights for two and a half hours, then cools down with 30 to 45 minutes on the StairMaster. His normal off-season workout day lasts from 7 a.m. to noon.

"I'm going into my 12th year, and I'm still explosive and still strong, so I must be doing something right," Rice says. "I don't think anything can hurt as badly as running that hill. If I can endure that, I can endure anything. Especially when you're running that hill yourself – your mind plays tricks on you, there's nobody around, you can quit if you want. Nobody's gonna know, but something inside says, 'Once you start quitting, that's it, it's over.' Because in a ball game, you're gonna be tired and hurting, you might feel like you don't have anything left, and what are you gonna do, quit? I never want to get into that quitting mode."

Rice has always been a fitness fiend, but he wasn't always as focused as he is now. As graceful as Rice looked to most observers early in his career, Farris saw several flaws. "From 1985 to 1987 he was a heavier player," Farris says. "He had an unconditioned body and a lag in his left leg. He had a lot of twitches and little things going on with his ankle and his knee. Jerry had good feet, but he was not a good technical player. It was ugly. That was the first thing I noticed, and I went right after that."

Rice came to Farris after the 1987 season. The 49ers were coming off a disappointing playoff defeat to the Vikings, a game in which Rice had been hobbled by an ankle sprain. Craig had been urging Rice to join his budding workout group for years, but Rice had resisted, because his first experience on the mountain trail was not a pleasant one. "Those guys kicked my butt," he recalls. "I said, 'Man, I can't believe this.' I thought I was in the best shape of my life as a youngster, and I felt strong. But those guys ran me into the ground."

Facing page and above: *Rice supplements his cardiovascular exercise with intense work in the weight room, where he hones his muscular physique.*

Says Craig: "We kind of scared him off a little bit. He ran it once, and then we didn't see him for a long time. He got intimidated by the hill. But I kept bugging him, telling him, 'You can take your career to a new level.' "

The next off-season, Rice began regular workouts on the track, on the football field, and in the weight room – but he wouldn't come near the hill. "The hill is the bible of life," Craig told him. "If you can conquer that hill, you can conquer anything."

Rice conquered it, and then some. "When he came back, he came back with a vengeance," Farris recalls. "He'd never been hurt like that before, and he was determined to master it." At first, Rice was happy making it up the hill in 18 or 19 minutes. He would eventually get to the point where he could run it in 16 minutes comfortably and 15 when going all out. He and Craig were like two kids playing a game of chicken, each pushing the other to unfathomable extremes, with Farris cracking the whip. "Man, it was uncontrollable," Farris says. "When I said, 'Go,' the track meet was on. We just went after each other. It's just the competitive mold that comes out." Says Craig: "We competed so hard against each other, Raymond had to keep us away. It was like an Olympic training center. We'd be at the track trying to run 200s at 25 or 26 seconds, and Jerry would be running 22 or 23. We'd say, 'Jerry, you're messing up the workouts.' He wanted to be the best, so now he trains to be the best. I have to admit it: He's now the King of the Hill."

As much as Rice believes in the workouts for professional reasons, the truth is he loves the competition. Williams recalls one track session in which Sanders and others came within a few inches of beating Rice at a 200-

meter dash. "One guy kind of started bragging about it," Williams recalls, "and Jerry looked at me and said, 'Watch this.' On the next 200, he took off like someone poured scalding water on him. He beat everyone by 20 yards." Rice has sometimes been beaten in selective races, but he always seems to win the last one. When the explosive Sanders is involved, Rice consciously tries to tire him out in the shorter sprints, then dominate him in later races.

Rice expects to be challenged by his NFL peers, but on one January day in 1994, Rice began feeling competitive vibes from Barry Bonds. True, Bonds is quite possibly the best baseball player on earth, but in Rice's eyes, he might as well have been competing with the world's best sumo wrestler. There was no way he was going to lose to a baseball player. "We were running 100s, and Barry Bonds, he was like trying to challenge me," Rice says. "I couldn't believe it. Raymond told me to ignore it. But stuff like that gets you going."

It seems bizarre that Rice would feel threatened by Bonds or anyone else, but it's part of what makes him special. As great as his career has been, Rice has never rid himself of the insecurity and fear of failure that date back to his rookie year.

"His insecurity is part of his strength, and I mean that in a respectful way," Williams says. "He's moved by fear. I think he has some insecurities about not being known as one of the best, about somebody saying there's a guy better than him, about not being valuable anymore."

During the nineties a handful of receivers have challenged Rice's supremacy: the Cowboys' Michael Irvin, Green Bay's Sterling Sharpe, Baltimore's Andre Rison, Buffalo's Andre Reed, and Minnesota's Cris Carter are the most prominent. All have put up impressive numbers and

Above: *Rice followed the lead of Craig (33), a star for the 49ers who ended his career with the Minnesota Vikings but remained close to his prodigy.* **Facing page:** *When others in his workout group make a run at Rice on the track, he shifts into another gear.*

116

"*It's like he's competing with time. He's gonna prove that he's gonna get better, that he's gonna beat the clock, and it's him lining up in front of age, and age is the cornerback covering him, and he's gonna beat it eight times out of 10. And it's incredible, but thank God he's ours.*"

Carmen Policy, President, 49ers

made eye-popping catches. Irvin, like Rice, has shone in big games. Rice knows all about the feats of his rivals, because he keeps tabs on them through the electronic and print media.

"If there's an article about a wide receiver, I'm gonna read it, because I know my name is in there somewhere," Rice says. "It's weird how it pops up. When I see one of the other guys mention something about my game, I'm looking to see if the guy really knows what I'm trying to do, just to see if he knows football."

Though he has been riled by his rivals' boasts in the past, Rice respects each of them. Besides, they all throw praise his way. Even the self-promoting Irvin once referred to Rice as "Jesus In Cleats." Rice usually gets angrier at NFL experts who rate him as anything less than the NFL's best; he still talks about one national magazine article that ranked him third in the NFL, behind Irvin and Rison, a few years back.

To keep his edge, Rice does more than stay in optimal physical shape. He's also a student of the game, as cornerback Eric Davis quickly learned. When Davis joined the 49ers as a second-round draft pick in 1990, he reported to training camp and was immediately assigned to cover Rice, who beat him so soundly it was embarrassing. But as Davis grew in ability and experience, Rice noted the improvement and attempted to apply it toward his own continuing education.

"When I first got there, my job in practice was to chase Jerry, and he'd have me turning all over the place," Davis recalls. "As time went on we developed a pretty good relationship, where he couldn't stand me covering him and I couldn't stand him catching the ball. When Jerry started coming up to me after practice and asking me questions, I knew I was making progress. He'd say, 'How did you get me on that one? How did you see that? How did you know I was doing this?' He always wanted to know how I had gotten him, and after I told him, he would never make that mistake again."

Says Rice: "I'm always trying to gather information from different people, because I might face that situation somewhere during the season. Eric would always come up with something new, and I think it made both of us into better players."

Another edge Rice carries into games is his incredible stamina. He constantly sizes up opponents to determine their physical and mental limits, patiently waiting for an opening. Defensive backs often believe they have a handle on Rice early in the game, sometimes even into the fourth quarter. Then, when he can see the fatigue in their eyes, he'll leave them in the dust. "It starts right before the game," Rice says. "That's the purpose for me, to try to wear this guy out, and towards the end just finish him off. I can see it, then I strike. You hear so many defensive backs say about me, 'He's the same in the fourth quarter as he is in the first quarter.' If you're not in the best shape of your life, if you haven't taken your body to that extra level of pain, you're not gonna be able to keep up."

To make sure he's a step ahead, Rice takes no chances. Always diet conscious, he recently hired a nutritionist. He often experiments with his playing weight and plans to slim down to 185 pounds for the 1996 season. Not that he tortures himself completely. "I always give myself one day a week to eat anything I want," he says. "That's the only way I can stay sane." Call it the Jerry Rice diet: pecan pie, ice cream, burgers, pizza … and six

Facing page and above: *Young receivers like the 49ers' J.J. Stokes (facing page) model themselves after Rice, who has made a career out of pushing himself.*

119

days a week of calorie-counting.

Rice is also big on visualization. The night before a game, he runs his routes over and over in his head, playing out different scenarios. He inevitably wakes up at three or four in the morning and repeats the sequence. He's too hyped up to sleep.

Most of all, Rice uses practice as a forum for his greatness. Most NFL players regard practice as a chore; to Rice, it is a laboratory for forming habits and reaffirming his edge. "He leaves no stone unturned in his preparation," says Denver Broncos coach Mike Shanahan, the 49ers' offensive coordinator from 1992 to 1994. "Every time he hits the practice field he's like a rookie trying to make the team. He practices the same way during the first week of the season as he does before the Super Bowl, and those work habits carry over to the rest of the team."

Rice has carried on Craig's tradition of running out each play in practice to the end zone. "It's all about training yourself," Rice says. "I think you practice the way you play." When Craig and Rice were teammates, mere practice wasn't enough. They'd make little side bets, throwing the ball to one another and attempting to catch it one-handed. Whoever dropped it first – usually after about 15 successful receptions apiece – would have to do pushups.

"I remember the first time I saw him take off a play," Davis says. "It was my third training camp [1992], and Shanahan was running a drill with Jerry running a clearing route on the backside. He was the decoy. Shanahan made them run the play five times in a row, and the linemen kept messing up. Five times in a row Jerry was open, and on the fifth time he was screaming profanities all the way back to the huddle. On the sixth one, Jerry jogged off the ball, and a lineman messed it up again. On no. 7, Jerry ran it wide open."

Because of his blistering drive, Rice is destined to go through his career without letting up. But Craig believes this same approach will bring Rice peace once his career is done. "When it's time for Jerry Rice to retire, he's gonna walk away with a smile," Craig says. "He gave his all on the practice field, in the locker room, on the hills, and on the playing field, so he won't walk away and say, 'I wish I had worked out a little harder.' He'll know he accomplished everything he possibly could have, and that's a special feeling."

"A lot of guys battle for 16 games. The thing that's different about Jerry is, he battles for 16 games plus 1,000 practices plus 150 days in the off-season."

**Steve Young,
Quarterback, 49ers**

Facing page: *Rice has a firm grasp on reality. He has proven that he knows what it takes to perform at a world-class level, year in, year out.*

Retracing his Steps

No matter how many long hills he climbs, no matter how many desserts he eschews, Jerry Rice can't play football forever. Someday – perhaps in a year, perhaps sometime after the turn of the century – he will hang up his cleats. Giving up the game he has loved and helped elevate will undoubtedly be traumatic for Rice, but he has a plan: He's going to spend time with his family, work with kids, kick back, maybe play a little golf....

Yeah, and when Madonna stops singing, she'll settle down to a life of knitting and bridge.

It's true that Rice has golf in his plans, but given his competitive nature, a round or two a week won't be enough to keep his interest. Instead, when he brings his Hall-of-Fame career to a close, the world's greatest receiver wants to try to qualify for the Professional Golfers Association (PGA) Tour.

"I've told Jackie and I've told my mother-in-law that when this is all over, I'm going to play on the PGA Tour," Rice says. "And they don't take me seriously right now. But that's something I'm really going to pursue. If I have the time and the right coaching, plus a little luck, you never know what I might be capable of."

Golf is a recent obsession for Rice. It came into his life in August of 1994. Before that, he cared so little for the game that upon receiving an expensive set of clubs as a gift, he gave them away. "Everything Jerry does he becomes a junkie," says his trainer, Ray Farris. "And yes, he's pretty good."

Rice has his handicap down to a 13, and he works on his game daily. Each morning during the season he stops by a driving range near the 49ers' practice facility and goes through a bag of balls before reporting to work. Then, when practice and meetings are over, he goes back to the range and hits some more. His chief off-season activities are workouts and golf. His wife, Jackie, calls him an addict. .

"He's a fanatic," she says. "I'm sorry they ever invented the game. He's obsessed with it. I don't know if I should admit this, but he talks about golf more than football. His dream is to one day play the tour. I tease him all the time: 'Gosh, if we have to live off your salary from golf, we'll all starve.' But when Jerry sets his mind on things he tries his best to achieve it, so I wouldn't put it past him. It's the perfect game for him, because it's challenging. This is something that has conquered him, so he wants to conquer it."

Typically, Rice became hooked because he couldn't tolerate failure. "It's the challenge of hitting that stationary white ball," he says. "What started me is when I tried it for the first time, I couldn't do it. And you say, 'Here I am, I'm athletic, I should be able to hit this ball.' So now it's something that drives me."

Can Rice pull it off? He has a tough road ahead, but there is precedent. John Brodie, the 49ers' star quarterback of the sixties and early seventies, went on to become a legitimate player on the senior tour.

But as intensely as Rice is moved by sports, his no. 1 priority is family. That point was driven home in May of 1996 when Jackie suffered severe complications while giving birth to the couple's third child, a daughter named Jada. Earlier pregnancies had produced daughter Jaqui (nine) and son Jerry Jr. (five), and everything had gone smoothly. But while Jada was born healthy, Jackie faced life-threatening surgery and spent a week and a half in extremely critical condition before beginning a long and draining recovery.

For Jerry, the experience will leave a permanent scar. "It's like nothing else is important in life anymore,"

Above and facing page: *Rice discovered golf in 1994 and quickly became obsessed, to the point where he is contemplating a post-football run at the PGA Tour.*

he says. "This has just been devastating. I have had a lot of challenges, but this is no doubt the ultimate. Football was always no. 1 in my life, but football is not no. 1 now. Sometimes I don't even think about football.

"It was a very traumatic situation. It puts life in perspective. You can't live for tomorrow. The thought had never crossed my mind that I wouldn't wake up the next day, or that I could lose one of my loved ones, until now. And that's something that's really scary."

Even before the scary incident took place, Jerry acknowledged the degree to which he depends upon his wife, saying: "Jackie's the backbone. She runs the household, makes sure the kids are taken care of. She does everything; I play football. I think, What would my life be like without this person? Man, it would be so chaotic and crazy."

Still, Rice is an attentive father, monitoring his children's educational progress, getting them dressed and taking them to school in the morning during the season. He meshes a nineties sensitivity with old-school sensibilities. He remembers the principles his parents taught him – treat everyone the way you want to be treated, never think of yourself as being above anyone else, and respect your elders no matter what. He and Jackie want their children to assimilate the same values.

"Jerry and I are both down-to-earth people," Jackie says. "Our belief is, no matter how much money or how many luxuries you have, you have to look at it like one day it could all be gone. We tell the kids, 'You do have things, but not everyone's as fortunate as you. And no matter how many nice things you have, that doesn't make you any better than anyone else.' We want to be able to give our kids the best of everything, but we also want to

instill in them that they're normal, just like any other kids. We try to do normal things. We go to McDonald's, play on the Playland and all that. People look at us like, 'What's a big star like Jerry Rice doing at McDonald's?' Hey, Jerry Rice likes Big Macs, too."

As a father, Jerry admits to some old-fashioned tendencies. "That's the way I was brought up," he says. "I didn't start going out until I was 17. I plan on standing there with my shotgun and everything."

Working with kids is in Rice's plans. He has quietly been active in charitable pursuits for some time. After scoring his 127th touchdown to break Jim Brown's record in 1994, Rice established the 127 Foundation, which supports organizations such as the March of Dimes, Big Brothers, Big Sisters, and the Omega Boys Club (located in San Francisco). To raise money for the foundation, Rice established an annual charity golf tournament that is now in its second year. "I get so much enjoyment out of giving – it's not about receiving all the time," says the NFL's greatest receiver. "That's where you really get rewarded in this life."

Rice has considered establishing a youth center to promote positive activities once his playing days are over. He also would consider coaching football at the youth or high school levels, "because if you can help one or two kids, point them in the right direction, that's a reward right there." Would Rice ever consider becoming an NFL coach? "No," he says, "because you can't really teach those guys anything. They don't want to listen."

Rice is ambivalent about whether he wants his son to play football. "If he wants to, I'm willing to help in any way possible," Rice says. "But it's a very violent sport, and he's going to have so many options. I'm not the type

Facing page: *Only two months after childbirth complications put her life in peril, Jackie shares a thankful moment with Jerry and new daughter, Jada.*
Above: *Jerry and his oldest daughter, Jaqui, catch some backyard rays with Sunshine, the family's rottweiler.*
Following pages: *Jerry Jr. strikes a pose for his parents, who hope he'll pursue a vocation less violent than football.*

of father who will try to groom his kids and get them into sports. But if he wants to play, I'll help him."

Jackie is less enthusiastic, saying, "Our little boy is such a computer whiz. We want him to do something more intellectual. I think Jerry's attitude is, 'That's why I'm taking all these bumps and bruises right now, so my kids won't have to.' "

Unlike some star athletes, Rice not only views himself as a role model but actively embraces the part. "I take that upon myself because kids are looking up to you, they're watching your every move, and they want to be just like you," Rice says.

Yet while Rice's endorsement profile has increased dramatically since Super Bowl XXIII, when he spoke out in frustration over his lack of commercial opportunities, he still ranks far behind many athletes who cultivate flashy off-the-field personas – Charles Barkley, Deion Sanders, and Shaquille O'Neal being examples.

"Let's face it, he's a great role model for kids," Jackie Rice says of her husband. "He hasn't done the drinking and the smoking and all that. He hasn't done the gold chains and the missing teeth. He's always gonna get overlooked because he's not as flamboyant and not as much of a buffoon as some of these other athletes. But the flashiness is what the media likes to hype up. His view now is, 'I'm not gonna change – so be it.' "

Rice has benefited from his long association with agent Jim Steiner of the St. Louis-based Sports Management Group, which has helped make Rice a recognizable face to many Americans. Among the major companies with which Rice has endorsement contracts are Nike, Breathe Right nasal strips, All-Sport/Pepsi, Visa,

Frito-Lay, Wheaties, Upper Deck trading cards, and SportsLine USA, an on-line service.

But Rice seems less interested in enhancing his public profile than he does in enjoying his private life. He has promised Jackie he won't ride his beloved Harley Davidson until his football career is over, but once that happens, look out – Rice, apparently, was born to be wild. "I feel so free when I ride it," he says. "You've got the wind blowing in your face, you're listening to the roar of the engine … It's just being free. That's what I want."

Not even Rice knows when he'll be allowed to climb aboard his chopper again. On one hand, he says he'll retire as soon as he feels he's starting to slip. But Rice won't rule out hanging on as a sort of elder statesman and possession receiver, even if his speed betrays him. "If I'm a possession guy and the young guys want me around to help them, that would probably keep me around," he says.

The 49ers hope to sign Rice to a lucrative contract extension through 2000, partly as a reward for years of loyal service, and partly because they know they'll never be able to replace him.

"You can't plan with Jerry," 49ers president Carmen Policy says. "How many years does he have left? I don't know. I'm thinking there's a painting somewhere in some attic that's going to grow older and older, and Jerry will stay younger and younger. You wonder, has he made a pact with some supernatural force?"

Though the competitive juices still rage like the Nile inside him, Rice claims to have acquired an inner peace during the past year or two. "I think he's come to face the fact that he's not gonna win the Super Bowl every year," Jackie says.

Facing page: *Whether they're shooting hoops at a plastic rim or battling in computer games, it's obvious that Jerry's competitive genes have been passed down to Jaqui and Jerry Jr.* **Above:** *To counteract their father's height advantage, Jaqui and Jerry Jr. have learned a few playground moves.*

"Before it was all about making everybody happy, and I think I focused so hard on that I forgot about myself," Jerry says. "You're gonna have some people that like you and some people that hate you, so why worry about it? People tried to change me when I first came out here. My former agent sent me to a speech therapist. Then I decided just to be myself. I'm just a country boy, and that's it. I'm happy with myself, with what I've achieved, with my family and with everything that's around me right now.

"Before, I would live and die football. Now there are more important things, like raising kids, my wife, being around my family."

There is, however, a slight complication. Rice may believe in his heart that he has conquered the madness that drove him to become the best, and his day-to-day reality may indeed be blissful. But there are deeply competitive ardors that surge through Rice's veins, instinctual forces that the rest of us will never comprehend. Even someone like Steve Young, a two-time NFL Most Valuable Player and a recent Super Bowl MVP, a fiery quarterback who knows Rice as well as almost any football player, is sometimes blown away by his teammate's desire.

Last January at Super Bowl XXX in Tempe, Arizona, Young and Rice joined other past Super Bowl MVPs for a pregame ceremony on the Sun Devil Stadium turf. The Dallas Cowboys and Pittsburgh Steelers were gathered on their respective sidelines, waiting to play in The Ultimate Game. Most of the former MVPs mingled with one another as they prepared to be introduced to the crowd, but Rice and Young stood alone and off to the side. Rice was fixated on the rival Cowboys. Young was watching Rice. "Then Jerry got a little tear in his eye," Young recalls, "and he looked at me and said, 'Never again.'"

What Rice meant was that, in his mind, he will never again allow the 49ers to fall short of a championship. But unwittingly, he spoke to a symbolic truth as well. Men will play football for hundreds of years, maybe thousands, and great players will come and go. But there will never be another competitor quite like Jerry Rice.

Jerry Rice

Facing page: Jaqui has no problem living the high life, but away from the trampoline, mom and dad want their children to regard themselves as normal kids. Following pages: Football's most famous hands have been passed down from Jerry to Jerry Jr.

"I was born with a very special gift that has taken years to develop, nurture, and refine. In my mind I know I can always get better, and each and every day I try to do something to reach my goals of being the best father, husband, friend, and yes ... football player.

My biggest fear is that someday I might fail, and that's what motivates me to keep my motor running at the highest level possible no matter what I'm doing, or when I'm doing it.

I've learned some very important lessons in the last few months and I realize now more than ever how really fragile life can be.

Sometimes we tend to move so fast we don't take the time to enjoy what is happening around us. No one is invincible and I truly understand how blessed I have been."

Jerry Rice

Jerry Rice: NFL Statistics

RECEIVING/*RUSHING*

YEAR	G/S	REC.	YDS.	AVG.	LONG	TD	*RUSH*	*YARDS*	*AVG.*	*TD*	*LONG*
1985	16/4	49	927	18.9	66t	3	6	26	4.3	1	15t
1986	16/15	86	1570	18.3	66t	15	10	72	7.2	1	18
1987	12/12	65	1078	16.6	57t	22	8	51	6.4	1	17
1988	16/16	64	1306	20.4	96t	9	13	107	8.2	1	29
1989	16/16	82	1483	18.1	68t	17	5	33	6.6	0	17
1990	16/16	100	1502	15.0	64t	13	2	0	0.0	0	0
1991	16/16	80	1206	15.1	73t	14	1	2	2.0	0	2
1992	16/16	84	1201	14.3	80t	10	9	58	6.4	1	26t
1993	16/16	98	1503	15.3	80t	15	3	69	23.0	1	43t
1994	16/16	112	1499	13.4	69t	13	7	93	13.3	2	28t
1995	16/16	122	1848	15.1	81t	15	5	36	7.2	1	20t
TOTAL	**172/159**	**942**	**15,123**	**16.1**	**96t**	**146**	**69**	**547**	**7.9**	**9**	**43t**

PLAYOFFS/RECEIVING/*RUSHING*

YEAR	G/S	REC.	YDS.	AVG.	LONG	TD	*RUSH*	*YARDS*	*AVG.*	*TD*	*LONG*
1985	1/1	4	45	11.3	20	0	0	0	0.0	0	0
1986	1/1	3	48	16.0	24	0	0	0	0.0	0	0
1987	1/1	3	28	9.3	13	0	0	0	0.0	0	0
1988	3/3	21	409	19.4	61t	6	3	29	9.7	0	21
1989	3/3	19	317	16.7	72t	5	0	0	0.0	0	0
1990	2/2	11	122	11.1	19	1	0	0	0.0	0	0
1992	2/2	14	211	15.1	36	1	1	9	9.0	0	9
1993	2/2	9	126	14.0	23	0	1	-9	-9.0	0	-9
1994	3/3	16	279	17.4	51t	4	1	10	10.0	0	10
1995	1/1	11	117	10.6	32	0	1	5	5.0	0	5
TOTAL	**19/19**	**111**	**1,702**	**15.3**	**72t**	**17**	**7**	**44**	**6.3**	**0**	**21**

PRO BOWL/RECEIVING/*RUSHING*

YEAR	G/S	REC.	YDS.	AVG.	LONG	TD	*RUSH*	YDS.	AVG.	TD	*LONG*
1987	1/1	1	13	13.0	13	0	1	6	6.0	0	6
1988	1/1	1	17	17.0	17	0	0	0	0.0	0	0
1989	INJURED/DID NOT PLAY										
1990	1/1	4	40	10.0	22	0	0	0	0.0	0	0
1991	1/1	3	62	20.7	49	0	0	0	0.0	0	0
1992	1/1	7	77	11.0	18	1	0	0	0.0	0	0
1993	1/1	4	78	19.5	48	0	1	3	3.0	0	3
1994	1/1	2	30	15.0	19	0	1	12	12.0	0	12
1995	INJURED/DID NOT PLAY										
1996	1/1	6	82	13.7	38	1	0	0	0.0	0	0
TOTAL	**8/8**	**28**	**399**	**14.3**	**49**	**2**	**3**	**21**	**7.0**	**0**	**21**

MILESTONE RECEPTIONS

1	at	Minnesota	(9-8-85)
100	at	Washington	(11-17-86)
200	vs	L.A. Rams	(12-27-87)
300	at	N.Y. Jets	(10-29-89)
400	at	Dallas	(11-11-90)
500	vs	New Orleans	(12-1-91)
509 *	vs	New Orleans	(12-1-91)
600	vs	Tampa Bay	(12-19-92)
700	vs	Houston	(12-25-93)
800	at	San Diego	(12-11-94)
875 **	vs	New Orleans	(11-26-95)
900	vs	St. Louis	(10-29-95)
941 ***	at	Atlanta	(12-24-95)

MILESTONE TOUCHDOWNS

1	at	Atlanta	(10-6-85)
50	vs	Washington	(11-21-88)
60+	vs	New Orleans	(11-6-89)
100	vs	Atlanta	(10-18-92)
101++	vs	Miami	(12-6-92)
127 +++	vs	L.A. Raiders	(9-5-94)
150	at	Miami	(11-20-95)

*   — broke 49ers' team record

**   — broke James Lofton's NFL record of 14,004 receiving yards

***   — broke Art Monk's NFL record of 940 receptions

+   — broke 49ers' team record for touchdown receptions

++   — broke Steve Largent's NFL record of 100 touchdown receptions

+++   — broke Jim Brown's NFL record of 126 touchdowns

G/S Games/Games started

REC. Number of receptions

YDS. Total yards

AVG. Average gains

LONG Longest gains

TD Touchdowns

RUSH Number of rushes

Index

Photographic references indicated in bold italics.

Acknowledgments

Created and Produced by Opus Productions Inc.

Author's Note

To begin, I am indebted to Jerry Rice, for helping to show me the relentless dedication required for success. I owe this opportunity to Janet Pawson and her colleagues at Athletes and Artists and to Mark Mulvoy, Bill Colson, Peter Carry, Steve Robinson, Mike Bevans, and the powers that be at Sports Illustrated. Among the colleagues who enhanced my work were Peter King, Rick Telander, Richard Weiner, Austin Murphy, Jarrett Bell, Ann Killion, Dave Guingona, and Brian Murphy. I truly appreciated the assistance of Jim Steiner and Kathy Fitzwater of Sports Management Group, as well as that of the San Francisco 49ers' public relations staff and of Chuck Profit at Mississippi Valley State. The contributions of clear thinkers Mike Fleiss and Jamie Williams were essential, as was the constant support of family and friends. This book was dignified by material gleaned from some of the sports world's most engaging and insightful interview subjects: Jackie Rice, Joe Montana, Eddie DeBartolo, Bill Walsh, Eric Davis, Jamie Williams, George Seifert, Carmen Policy, Steve Young, Mike Shanahan, Mike Holmgren, Roger Craig, Kevin Smith, Dwight Clark, Raymond Farris, Eddie B. Rice, Archie Cooley, John Taylor, Deion Sanders, Harris Barton, and Harry Sydney. Finally, special thanks to those who serve as the purest form of motivation: Stephen, Susan, and Elizabeth Silver, and Mark Tourgeman; the Goyette Family; and Leslie, Dr. J, and Natalie.

Michael Silver

Opus Productions Inc.

President/Creative Director: Derik Murray
Vice President, Production: David Counsell
Design Director: Don Bull
Visual Coordinator: Joanne Powers
Photography Coordinator: Colette Aubin
Electronic Art: Joseph Llamzon, Guylaine Rondeau

Chief Financial Officer: Jamie Engen
General Counsel/Photo Permissions: Ruth Chang
Marketing Manager: David Attard
Sales Representative: Chris Richardson
Office Manager: Catherine Palmer

Vice President/Publishing Director: Marthe Love
Senior Editor: Brian Scrivener
Executive Publishing Coordinator: Wendy Darling
Publishing Associate: Jennifer Love
Editorial Coordinator: Michelle Hunter
Publicity Coordinator: Gillian Hurtig
Publishing Assistants: Iris Ho, Allie Wilmink

Opus Productions would like to thank the following:

Sports Management Group: Jim Steiner, Kathy Fitzwater

San Francisco 49ers: Dwight Clark, Dave Rahn

St. Martin's Press: Neal Bascomb, Holly Bash, Shawn Coyne, David Kaye, Sally Richardson, Joe Rinaldi, Phil Schwartz, Matthew Shear

National Football League Properties, Inc: Matt Marini

Jim Steiner with Jaqui and Jerry Jr.
ROBERT BECK

Opus Productions would like to extend a special thank you to the Rice family:
Jerry, Jackie, Jerry Jr., Jaqui, Jada, Eddie B., and Joe Nathan Sr.; Gloria Mitchell Campbell and Charles Campbell; Toni Mitchell and Marilyn Davis.

Opus Productions would like to acknowledge the following for their assistance and support:
the staff of B. L. Moor High School • Robert Beck • Catherine Bennett • Bill Cartwright • Roger Craig • Trevor Doull, Sportsbook Plus • Sharyn Duffy • Raymond Farris, All Season Training • Linda Goodman, Don Ogden, Gayle Robson, Supreme Graphics • Carolyn Hoskins • Joe Jacobs • Thom Klaus • Cliff Mears • Robert Mizono • Lisa Morrison • John Nicolls • Marc Perman • Cliff Pickles, North South Travel • Charles Prophet, Mississippi Valley State University • Shawn and Sonovia Rogers • Tom Roster • Paula Wellings

Photography Credits

Cover: ROBERT MIZONO • Rice Family Photo Session: ROBERT BECK
BECK, ROBERT: front endsheet, 106, 108, 109, 112, 113, 114-15, 117, 118, 119, 121, 124, 125, 126, 127, 128-29, 130, 131 both, 132, 133, 134, 138, 144, back endsheet; Allsport/BELLO, AL: 103; CARLICK, JEFF/Sportschrome: 64; DRAKE, BRIAN/Sportschrome: 66-67; Allsport/DUNN, STEPHEN: 72 FOGEL, RIC/Bernhardt Sports Photography: 92-93; IOOSS, JR., WALTER/Sports Illustrated: 56 above; JACOBS, JOSEPH: 1, 9, 19, 39, 62-63 all, 69, 107, 123, 141; KANE, RICH/Sportschrome: 71; MESSERSCHMIDT, AL: 8, 54, 78-79, 82, 83, 102; MILLAN, MANNY/Sports Illustrated: 18; MILLER, PETER READ/ Sports Illustrated: 104-5; MIZONO, ROBERT: cover, 6, 122, 136-137; PERLSTEIN, MARK: 26, 27, 28, 29, 30-31, 33, 34 both, 37; ©1996 PFLEGER, MICKEY/Sports California: 4-5, 14-15, 17, 48, 49, 50, 52-53, 55, 57, 58-59, 68, 74 all, 76, 79 right, 80, 97, 100-101, back cover; Allsport/POWELL, MIKE: 94 below left, 99; Courtesy of Rice Family Collection: 2, 21, 23; Courtesy of ROGER CRAIG: 116; ROSTER, TOM: 20, 22, 25, 110-11; Sportschrome: 81 above left; The Sporting News: 35; TRINGALI, JR., ROB/Sportschrome: 90, 91; ZAGARIS, MICHAEL: 10, 11, 12, 36, 38, 40, 41, 42, 43, 44, 47, 56 below, 60, 73, 75, 81 above right and below left and right, 84, 85, 87, 88-89, 89 right, 94 above right and left and below right, 95